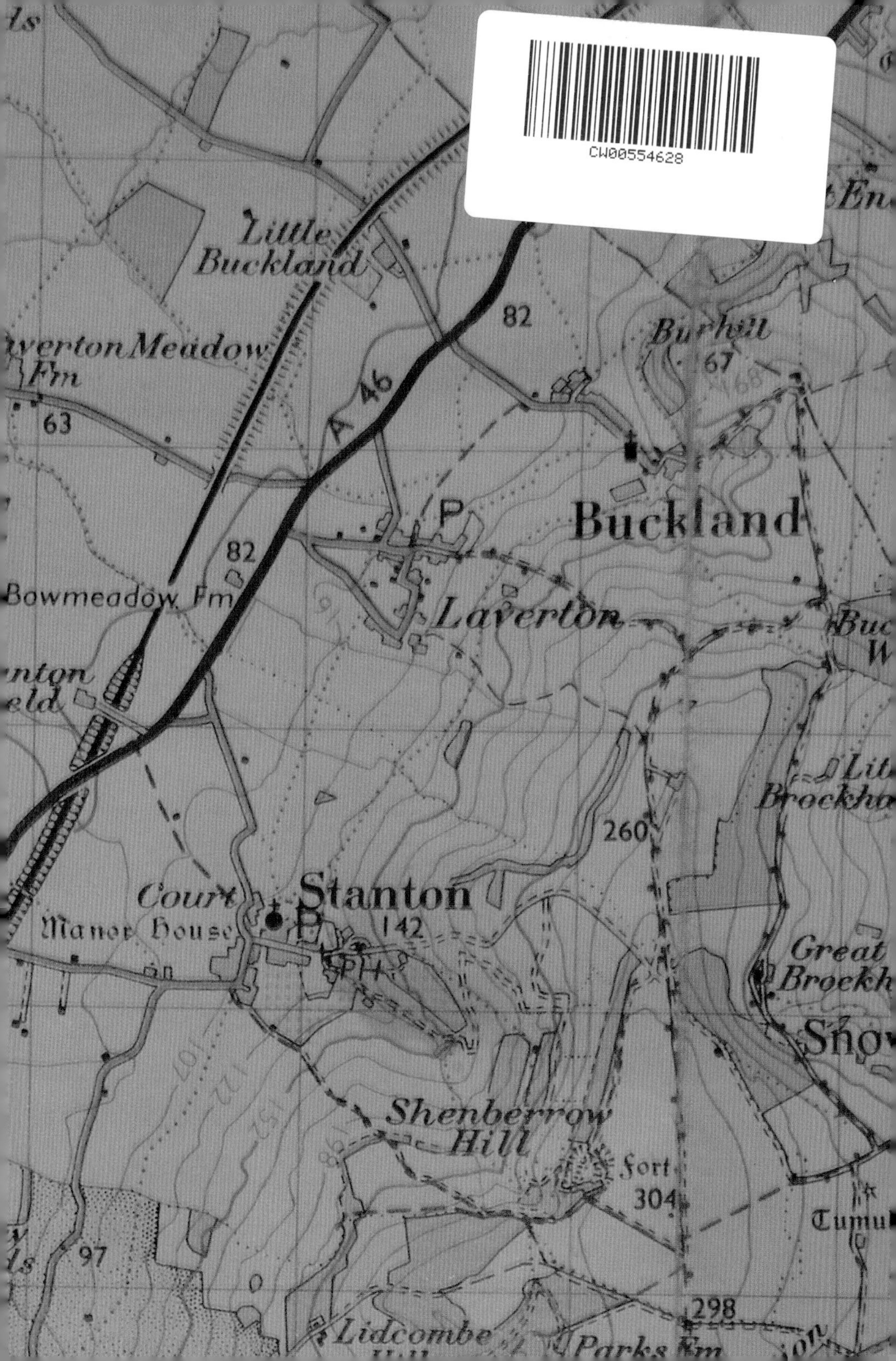
Little Buckland
Fm
63
82
A 46
Burhill
67
Buckland
P
82
Bowmeadow Fm
Laverton
260
Court
Stanton
Manor House
P
142
PH
Shenberrow Hill
Fort
304
97
Lidcombe
298

A SCHOOL IN THE COUNTRY

Didbrook School

in the Parish of Stanway, in the Cotswolds

Gloucestershire

by
Jillian R Mann

The School has also been known as:

From 1879 or earlier as Didbrook Mixed School
From 1894 or earlier as Didbrook C of E School No 25421 and/or 103
From August 30th 1921 as Didbrook Council School No 103
From April 1st 1935 as Stanway Council School
From April 1st 1945 as Stanway County School
From January 12th 1954 as Stanway County Primary School No 2083
From some time between 1970 and 1983 as Didbrook County Primary
School and later as Didbrook Primary School

Published by
REARDON PUBLISHING
PO Box 919, Cheltenham, Glos, GL50 9AN.
Website: www.reardon.co.uk
Tel: 01242 231800
email: reardon@bigfoot.com

Copyright © 2011

Written and Compiled
by
Jillian R Mann

Layout and Design
by
Nicholas Reardon

ISBN 1 87419252 9
ISBN (13) 9781874192527

All Royalties from this book will benefit
Isbourne Valley School and Didbrook Church

A School in the Country- Illustrations and their Legends

The illustrations were, unless otherwise indicated, obtained from the Archive of Didbrook School, by permission of its Head teacher, Mr D Ogden and the Governing body (now Isbourne Valley School).

Printed Through
World Print Ltd

A SCHOOL IN THE COUNTRY

CONTENTS

FOREWORD

Jill Mann's book on Didbrook School does not merely chronicle the history of the institution, but supplies abundant personal anecdotes of past pupils, and describes the geographical, social, political and economic circumstances within which the school operated from the early 19th century to the present.

As anybody with experience of this type of research will be aware, the amount of labour involved in compiling so accurate and detailed an account of the school's history, with its many statistics, is vast and indeed, as Americans say, awesome.

But by so skilfully setting the school in its local context, she has illuminated the history of Didbrook and the surrounding parishes, especially Stanway and Hailes, in a way that has not been done before, and has explained how the inhabitants of this part of north Gloucestershire have lived their lives and interacted with events in the wider world over the last two centuries.

Those who love Didbrook School and this county therefore owe her an enormous debt of gratitude for a work of the highest quality which, for interest and informativeness, will not easily be surpassed.

Wemyss

PREFACE

I am grateful to the School's Governors for giving me access to the Log Books and Admissions registers of Didbrook School, the first Log Book of Stanway School and the Minutes of Governors meetings of Didbrook School. Access to the second Log Book of Stanway School was provided by Gloucestershire Archives. Much of the information in this book was derived from the Log Books and whenever a direct quotation is made from these documents, it is shown in italics. I must also thank the staff of Gloucestershire Archives, Birmingham Archives and Heritage, Birmingham Central Library and the National Archives at Kew, for their unfailing help and encouragement. The illustrations were, unless otherwise indicated, obtained from the Archive of Didbrook School, by permission of its Head teacher, Mr D Ogden and the Governing body (now Isbourne Valley School).

I would like to thank the many people who have contributed information, photographs and helpful criticism for this book. They include Mrs Hilda Archer, Mr Francis and Mrs Dorothy Andrews, Mr Philip Andrews, Miss Sarah Andrews, Mrs Betty Blayney (née Wright), Mrs Libby Brett, Mr Philip and Mrs Susan Boreham Mrs Jane Brooks, Mrs Sheena Brown (née Nightingale), Mrs Wendy Butler (née Sadler), Mr Andrew Clark, Mrs Doreen Clark, Miss Jessica Edmonds, Mrs Barbara Edward and Mrs Carol Harris (Winchcombe Folk and Police Museum), Mr Mark Farmer, Mrs Elizabeth Fenton (née Holmes), Mrs Susan Firkins (née Mann), Mrs Morna Fisher (née Kathleen Morna Horlick), Mr David Gregory, Mrs Julie Harris (née Beard), Mrs Sandra Harris (née Foster), Mr Bruce and Mrs Daphne Hayward, Mr Chris and Mrs Sally Higgins, Mrs Susan Hillmore, Mr Horace Holmes, Mr Albert (Bert) Hughes, Mr Tim and Mrs Stella Idiens, Mrs Pat Lewis, Mrs Ann Lyon (née Holmes), Mr Philip Mann, Mr Bryan Markwell, Mrs Lesley Marriott, Mrs Doreen Nurden (née Bourne), Mr David Ogden, Mrs Sheila Parkes, Mr Tim Petchey (Winchcombe Railway Museum), Mrs Pam Righton, Mr Joel Roberts, Mrs Marian Roberts (née Vellender), Mr John Russell, Mrs Ann Tilley (née Sadler), Mr David Sanders, Mrs Christina Shaw, Mr Toby Shaw, Miss Joyce Simpson, Mrs Joyce Stevens, Mr Gareth Thomas, Mr Geraint Thomas, Mrs Margaret Varnish (née Mann), Mr Alan Vickers, Mr Ian and Mrs Margaret Warmington, Mrs Alison Whiston, Mrs Nancy Whitcombe (née Simpson), Mrs Georgette Williams (née Horlick), Lord Wemyss, Mr Seymour Wilcox and Mr Glyn Wright.

The various archives contain two spellings for the neighbouring village, Hailes and Hayles. Except where direct quotations are made, Hailes is used.

Events and observations seen or experienced by the author are described in the first person.

I have tried to acknowledge everyone who has provided information, photographs or other assistance in the production of this book and apologise for any omissions or inaccuracies.

This book is dedicated to my Parents and Uncle Frank

JRM

INTRODUCTION

Education in England and Wales

The first school in Great Britain was the Cathedral School in Canterbury, which was founded in AD 597 to provide an education for the choirboys there. Subsequently many similar Cathedral Schools were founded and also, from the 13th and 14th centuries, a number of (university) colleges. One of the earliest Grammar Schools was Gloucester Grammar School, founded in 1410 [1] and Winchcombe's first Grammar School was founded in 1519, paid for from the estate of Lady Joan Huddleston of Sudeley Castle [2].

The early educational institutions were generally for boys and charged fees, so the poor remained uneducated and the only girls to be educated were taught by privately employed governesses or priests. However, in 1698 the Society for Promoting Christian Knowledge (SPCK) was established and funded many schools from donations, aiming to have one school for the poor in every parish.

During the 18th century, non-conformists also set up schools. In addition, Industrial Schools were established for children working in factories who were taught reading, writing, spinning, sewing, gardening etc, and their work was sold to defray some of the costs of their education. But many children were at work throughout Monday to Saturday and therefore Sunday Schools were started; one of the first was set up in Sooty Lane, Gloucester, in 1780 by Robert Raikes, an associate of William Wilberforce.

Samuel Whitbread's Parochial Schools Bill of 1807 was a first attempt to establish parochial schools in England and Wales. It met fierce opposition in the Commons and was rejected in the Lords. Curtis wrote 'The governing classes viewed with suspicion any attempt to diffuse education amongst the ranks of the poor....' and '....the Church was firmly opposed to any form of religious instruction of an undenominational character....' [1]. Likewise, Brougham's Parochial Education Bill of 1820 which aimed to put schools where they were needed, with buildings paid for by manufacturers and salaries from a tax on the gentry and the rates, with parents contributing 2d or 4d per child per week fees, was also rejected.

Despite these setbacks, through the Church of England and non-conformist churches, public subscriptions, private benefactors, various endowments, and parental contributions in the form of fees, during the 19th century the number of children able to receive education steadily rose. In 1820 it was about 700,000 (1/15 of the child population), in 1832 it was about 1,030,000 in non-endowed schools and 165,000 in endowed schools, and the numbers continued to rise thereafter.

The Reform Bill of 1832 provided the first government grants towards the cost of building school houses (which provided a house for the teacher and a classroom) and from 1839 Her Majesty's Inspectors were introduced to oversee schools.

Throughout the 19th and early 20th centuries, children were very much part of the work force, upon which the Industrial Revolution and family finances depended. Despite Robert Peel's Factory Act of 1802, which restricted hours worked by children to 12 per day, and his Factory Act of 1815, which restricted employment to children aged over 10 years, and other legislation, children continued to work long hours, so found it hard to attend school during the week - hence the success of Sunday Schools.

Education in a rural setting

Much of the early legislation related particularly to children living in towns, but child labour was equally important in country areas so, even when a school was available, children often attended irregularly. Like many other country schools that were originally set up in the 18th and 19th centuries and paid for by the local landowners, Didbrook and Stanway Schools were primarily intended for the children of the workers on the estates and others living in the estates' villages. They also catered for some children from surrounding areas. Throughout their existence they have received financial support and patronage from the Lord of the Manor and his family.

Didbrook and Stanway are two of a number of pretty villages just below the Cotswold escarpment in rural north Gloucestershire. They have in common a water supply from many springs, fertile land in the valley, wooded slopes on the escarpment which yield timber, and good grazing on the hills above. These features made them suitable for sheep farming and other agricultural purposes. The houses were built in the gold-coloured Cotswold stone obtained from local quarries, or with timber frames from the woods, filled in with mud and wattle or brickwork. While they are now popular with tourists, including those who enjoy walking along the Cotswold Way which passes through the parish, these villages felt remote before motor transport was introduced.

The villages of Stanway, Hailes and Toddington are all approximately one mile from Didbrook. The closest small towns, Winchcombe and Broadway, are three and five miles away respectively. All the larger towns which surround Didbrook are ten to twelve miles away - Cheltenham, Tewkesbury, Evesham, Chipping Campden, Moreton-in-Marsh, Stow-on-the-Wold and Bourton-on-the-Water. In the 19th century children generally went to school on foot, as few parents had any other form of transport. Also, throughout most of the 20th century the children walked or bicycled to school, often long distances along country roads and footpaths, through woods and across fields.

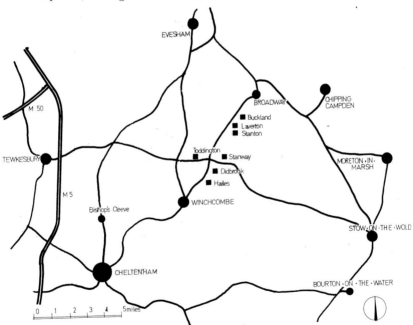

Diagram showing the position of Didbrook and of the other villages under the Cotswold escarpment, and the surrounding towns, drawn by Mr EM Foster.

The opening in 1906 of the Great Western Railway line between Honeybourne and Cheltenham provided public transport from Toddington Station or Hailes Halt and this was used by those children who gained entry to the Grammar and Technical Schools in Cheltenham. In the 1950s a bus service was started to take children to schools in

Tewkesbury too. Unfortunately in 1960, due to their unprofitability, the railway line's passenger services were closed and an infrequent bus service was substituted. Later Dr Beechings's cuts also closed the line to freight. It was not until well after the Second World War (WW II) that many families had their own cars. Therefore, apart from those who were able to gain places at Grammar or Technical Schools, until the 1950s most of the children living in Didbrook, Stanway and the adjacent villages had all their primary and secondary education in the village schools.

Demographic changes in Didbrook and the surrounding area over two centuries

The population data gathered in the national censuses from 1801 to 2001 for Didbrook and the neighbouring villages, and the nearest small town of Winchcombe, are shown in Table 1 [3-13]. The changes in acreage of the civil parishes resulted from alterations in boundaries and amalgamations of some of the civil parishes. The figures show overall growth in the total population in the area over the two centuries (3663 persons in 1801 to 5622 in 2001), and a rural to urban shift of population. The population of the small town of Winchcombe increased from 1888 to 4379, while the overall population in the villages decreased from 1775 to 1243. The exception is Toddington, where the population increased (268 to 416) following movement of its boundaries and much new building during the 20th century. Thus, it was in the smaller villages, Didbrook, Hailes, Stanway, Wormington, Stanton, Buckland and Laverton where the population actually decreased (1835 to 1093 persons). The loss of Pinnock and Hyde to the Cotswold District in 1951 does not alter these conclusions, because this locality has, throughout the 19th and 20th centuries, had a very small population, being largely meadows and woodland. These changes partly account for the closure, or threatened closure, of several of the village schools over the years.

Not only did the number of people living in the villages change, so did their socio-economic structure. In the 19th century, the majority of people lived as tenants in properties owned by the local landowners of the large estates, and the farmers were also tenants of the estates. Most people worked directly for the landowner, or indirectly, for example as labourers for farmers. However, during the 20th century, the estates at Toddington (which included most of Hailes), Stanton and Buckland were sold and the houses and cottages within them are now largely owner-occupied, often by relatively wealthy 'incomers' who have, or did have, town-based occupations elsewhere. Many no longer have children of school age.

Table 1. ACREAGES AND NUMBER OF PEOPLE RECORDED IN THE PARISHES IN THE CENSUSES OF 1801 to 2001

Parish	Didbrook		Pinnock & Hyde		Hailes		Stanway $		Wormin-ton		Stanton		Buckland $		Todding-ton		Winchcombe	
	Acres	No	Acr	No	Acr	No	Acr	No	Acr	No	Acr	No	Acr	No	Acr	No	Acr	No
1801	1528*	254	1050	125	1447	111	3390	342	532	91	1650	256	2275	328	1857	268	5700	1888
1811		201		42		122		403		81		244		324		261		1936
1821		291		33		136		415		83		269		382		355		2240
1831		240		47		123		401		96		293		403		290		2514
1841		292		61		120		384		73		319		377		229		2613
1851		149		29		90		359		62		307		368		189		2824
1861		182		50		102		378		79		280		355		153		2937
1871		200		39		91		335		86		282		354		221		2993
1881		215		29		57		307		94		269		283		212		2834
1891		205		30		63		310		79		265		259		236		2868
1901	536*	112	2359*	110	1447	82	3860*	332	532	79	1818*	275	2275	283	1828*	202	6720*	2699
1911		151		85		111		312		82		343		283		333		2930
1921		145		100		88		280		78		302		266		315		2741
1931		160		70		83		302		67		309		240		299		2546
1951	-	-	-	-	-	-	4519*	412	-	-	2350*	249	2275	241	3172*	449	5516*	2781
1961	-	-	-	-	-	-		415	-	-		262		219	2853*	381		3047
1971	-	-	-	-	-	-		348	-	-		230		206		396		4070
1981	-	-	-	-	-	-		347	-	-		223		213		390		4754
1991	-	-	-	-	-	-		322	-	-		222		247		418		4835
2001	-	-	-	-	-	-		354	-	-		217		256		416		4379

$ Buckland includes Laverton. Stanway includes Coscombe, Stumps Cross and Taddington and, from 1951, also Didbrook and Hailes.

* Boundary changes in 1901 altered the acreages (and consequently the populations) of some parishes. Boundary changes in 1951 put Pinnock and Hyde in Cotswold District, and Didbrook and most of Hailes in Stanway Parish, raising its acreage to 4519. Also in 1951, Wormington was included in Stanton Parish, Toddington's acreage increased to 3172 (but in 1961 fell to 2853) and Winchcombe's acreage rose to 5561.

SOURCES

1. Population Tables of 1801-1851, contained within Census of Great Britain 1951, County of Gloucester, Volume I, published by W Clowes and Sons, London, 1852 for HMSO
2. Census Tables of Population 1801-1901, copied from the Victorian History of the County of Gloucestershire, Volume II
3. Census of England and Wales Vol I HMSO London, 1912
4. Census of England and Wales 1921 County of Gloucester, HMSO London, 1923
5. Census of England and Wales 1931 County of Gloucester, Part I, HMSO London, 1933
6. Census of England and Wales 1951 County Report, Gloucestershire, HMSO London, 1954
7. Census of England and Wales 1961 County Report, Gloucestershire, HMSO London, 1964
8. Census of England and Wales 1971 County Report, Gloucestershire, HMSO London, 1973
9. Census 1981 OPCS Monitor. Ward and Civil Parish Monitor, Gloucestershire, 1984
10. Census 1991 OPCS Monitor. Ward and Civil Parish Monitor, Gloucestershire, 1993 (obtained via the National Statistics website: www.statistics.gov.uk)
11. Census 2001, obtained on line via www.ons.gov.uk/census/get-data/index.html

All Census data are Crown copyright material which is reproduced with the permission of the Controller of HMSO

In contrast, the Wemyss family continues to own and manage the Stanway estate, which includes Stanway and Didbrook villages and the hamlets of Coscombe and Taddington. Most of the properties are rented from the estate, the owner-occupied properties mostly being those previously owned by the Church or Gloucestershire County Council. The policies of the Wemyss family have included trying to preserve the ancient buildings, woodland and other features, as well as a range of rural industries in the villages. They let the cottages at moderate rents, giving priority to people who can contribute rural skills and have family connections with the villages. Most of the children of their tenants have attended Didbrook School or, in the earlier years, Stanway School.

Socio-economic evolution within Stanway Parish
(Stanway, Didbrook, Taddington, Coscombe and Hailes)
during the 19th and 20th centuries

Census data [3-14] reveal that during the two centuries the total number of inhabitants decreased, and also the proportion who were children. In 1851 there were 592 inhabitants, 37% aged less than 16 years, 56% aged 16 to 65 years and 14% aged over 65 years. By 2001 the total population had dropped to 354, only 24% being aged less than 16 years, 64% aged 16 to 65 years and 12% aged over 65 years.

Also, some properties in Stanway Parish were lost (for example, due to fire, or building works which combined pairs of very small cottages into single bigger ones). But some new houses were built, resulting in little overall change to the number of houses or households. The 1851 census documented 136 houses and those of 1901, 1951 and 2001 showed respectively 131, 127 and 144 households. Overcrowding was a feature of family life in the 19th and early 20th centuries. In 1851 many small cottages, which generally had only one to three bedrooms, housed families of over eight inhabitants. However, falling birth rates and other factors in the 20th century reduced the average number of people per house or household; it was 4.61 in 1851, 4.85 in 1901, 3.24 in 1951 and 2.46 in 2001.

In 1851 the predominant occupations of people living in these villages were related to agriculture. There were 19 farmers, some with a very small acreage which they farmed themselves, but others had over 100 acres and employed over 10 labourers. Altogether, at least 62% of the working population was engaged in work on the land. These people included some 145 farm labourers, (mostly men and boys, but also a few women and girls), wagoners and carters, shepherds, foresters,

Table 2. SOCIO-ECONOMIC FEATURES ILLUSTRATED BY THE 2001 CENSUS

Feature	Stanway		Stanton		Buckland		Toddington		Winchcombe	
Total Population	354		217		256		416		4379	
Age (years)	No	%	No	%	No	%	No	%	No	%
0-15	86	24	27	12	28	11	68	16	703	16
16-65	226	64	133	62	164	64	287	68	2548	58
Over 65	42	12	57	26	64	25	61	16	1128	26
Dwellings	No	%		%		%	No	%	No	%
Occupied	144		112		116		164		2007	
Unoccupied	7		5		3		0		36	
Second homes	3	2	25	18	20	14	6	4	46	2
Households *	%		%		%		%		%	
Average No Persons per household	2.46		1.94		2.21		2.54		2.17	
Rented	59		31		20		20		25	
With long-term ill person $	54		29		14		7		12	
With central heating & bathroom #	79		88		88		93		90	

*Household = Occupied dwelling
$ Defined as one or more persons with limiting long-term illness
# Defined as with central heating and sole use of bath or shower and toilet

gardeners, a poultryman, gamekeepers, grooms and a farm bailiff. About 13% of workers did domestic work, and there were also blacksmiths, carpenters, a sawyer, a builder, a slater and plasterer, masons, roadmen, a surveyor of roads, a foreman on turnpike roads, grocers, bakers, shoe makers, dressmakers, silk and cord winders, glovers, school mistresses and a curate. Nearly all of these residents worked within the farms and villages [14].

Agriculture remained the principal occupation of the villagers until the mid-20th century when farming gradually became mechanised. The first tractor in the Parish was probably the Allis Chalmers bought in 1937 by W Mann and Sons of Stanway. Further use of machines to replace horse power then occurred rapidly, partly because of WW II. Consequently, the need for manual agricultural workers decreased. A survey in 2010 by the author revealed that by the end of the first decade of the 21st century there were only 7 farmers and about 7 farm labourers still living and working in Stanway Parish. There were also some 7 gardeners and 2 estate workers. Additional casual agricultural labour from outside the Parish was employed at busy times, such as lambing and harvest.

The national census of 2001 [13] confirmed that most of the 182 residents of the Parish aged between 16 and 74 years who were employed were not working in agriculture. Many travelled outside their villages to work, an average distance of 12.82 km. Nevertheless, 67 people worked at, or within walking distance of their home. The author's survey of 2010 indicated that these included the farmers and other workers on the land referred to above and also a gamekeeper, a plant breeder, bed and breakfast proprietors, domestic cleaners, a laundress, a blacksmith, a riding school proprietor and other equestrian workers, a dog breeder and kennel man, secretaries, writers, artists, a musician, computer workers, a caretaker, an architect, and a photographer. Those who did much or most of their work outside the villages included drivers, builders, plumbers, a quarryman, bartenders, a financier, a mechanic and antique dealers.

The census of 2001 also revealed some of the ways in which Stanway Parish and the neighbouring parishes changed over the 20th century, so that they came to differ from each other in a number of respects (Table 2). Compared with Stanton, Buckland, Toddington and Winchcombe, Stanway Parish had the youngest population, 24% being aged less than 16 years, and far more households where there were one or more persons with limiting long-term illness (54%). Also, the percentage of households living in rented accommodation was much higher in Stanway (59%) than in the other parishes and the percentage with separate bathrooms somewhat lower (79%). Moreover, in Stanton and Buckland 18% and 14% respectively of the dwellings were second homes, whereas in Stanway, Toddington and Winchcombe the figures were only 2% to 4%.

Personal memories of Didbrook School

For almost a century Didbrook School has played an important role in the life of my family. Both of my parents, William (Bill) Mann and Vera Austin, were pupils there and so were Uncle Frank, my sisters Susan and Margaret, my brother Philip and I. When Bill and Frank attended their father, William Mann, was farming at Farmcote with his wife Rose. They started school in 1916 or 1917 when they were aged 6 and 5 years respectively. The two little boys walked about two miles to Didbrook each morning, down the track beside the wood to Hailes and then across the fields to Didbrook (see the map). In the evenings they returned the way they had come although, especially in bad weather, were sometimes met at Hailes by their father with his pony and trap.

Bill and Frank Mann circa 1915 (provided by JR Mann)

Although she was three months younger than Dad (they were both born in 1910) Mum started at Didbrook School some time before he did, probably because her journey was much easier. She lived at Lower Hailes Farm, where her parents, Ernest and Emma Austin, were tenants. Their second daughter, Avis, also probably went to Didbrook School for a short time, but Howard, Phyllis and Selwyn started their education at Stanton School after the family moved to the Manor Farm there in 1917.

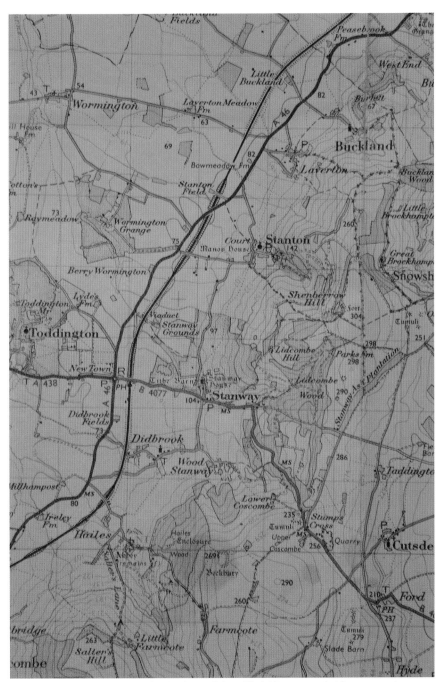

- 17 -

Mum could recollect the day that Dad and Uncle Frank first attended Didbrook School and were introduced to the other pupils, and how bedraggled they were on rainy mornings.

My personal recollections of Didbrook School date from the summer of 1944, just after my fifth birthday. I was taken there by my mother, who introduced me to Miss Last, who was in charge of the 'Little Room', for infants. This was separated from the 'Big Room', for older children, by a moveable screen. The two classrooms were both within what is now the open hall / activity area, and the only other accommodation consisted of the cloakrooms and lavatories and a small kitchen. Heating was provided by iron stoves which, even when well-stoked with coal, were not really up to the task of keeping us warm. The canteen was built around the time that I first started at the school.

'Three little girls from School are we...' Sue, Jill and Margaret Mann, 1947
(photograph taken by John Horlick, provided by Mrs Morna Fisher)

The walls of the Little Room were decorated by a home-made frieze consisting of a pictorial illustration of the alphabet. Using this, each morning we chanted 'A is for Apple', 'B is for Ball ', 'C is for Cat', 'D is for Dog', 'E is for Egg...........' There were also all the tables from 2 to 12 which we chanted daily ' 2 times one is 2 , 2 times 2 is 4, 2 times 3 is 6 ....' Everyone quickly became word-perfect. Miss Last seated me at one of the little double wooden desks next to David Turpitt. We were each given a piece of chalk and a slate on which we wrote our spellings and sums. We later progressed to pencil and paper.

Each day began with the morning service conducted for the whole school in the Big Room by the headmistress, Mrs Ada Holdsworth. Miss Last played the piano for the hymns and often did a reading. Afterwards the infants returned to the Little Room for their lessons. Except in severe weather, we spent the mid-morning break in the playground and at lunchtime some of us who lived nearby went home for our meals. The others ate the meal cooked by Mrs Brewin (Glyn Wright has fond memories of semolina pudding) or had their sandwiches in the classrooms. After lunch the infants lay down on canvas camp beds for their rest before the final teaching session of the day.

We were still at war in 1944 and some of the large number of evacuees who were billeted in the area still attended the school. I remember girls from London teaching us Cockney playground songs and games, such as 'Oranges and lemons' and 'London Bridge is falling down', while we taught them 'The farmer needs a wife'. One of the evacuees once confided in me that she was the product of a mixed marriage, by which she meant that one parent was a Protestant and the other a Roman Catholic. This had clearly been a problem for her which I found hard to understand, although even then I was aware that the presence in Didbrook at that time of both a Church and a Wesleyan Chapel sometimes caused awkwardness.

I was thrilled, of course, in 1950 to move on to Pate's Grammar School for Girls in Cheltenham, but never lost touch with Mrs Holdsworth and Miss Last, and have many happy memories of my time at Didbrook School and am grateful for the good start they gave me.

This book

The purpose of this book is to illustrate the development of education in rural England during the 19th and 20th centuries by describing the history of Didbrook School (and also of Stanway School with which it was amalgamated in 1921) alongside the changes in education and society in the country as a whole. The school was closed in July 2008, but was amalgamated with Toddington School and reopened in September 2008 as Isbourne Valley School.

SOURCES

1.   Curtis SJ. History of Education in Great Britain, 7th Edition, University Tutorial Press, London, 1967.
2.   Donaldson DN. Winchcombe. A history of the Cotswold borough. Wychwood Press, Charlbury, Oxfordshire, 2001.
3.   Population Tables of 1801-1851, contained within Census of Great Britain 1951, County of Gloucester, Volume I, published by W Clowes and Sons, London, 1852 for HMSO
4.   Census Tables of Population 1801-1901, copied from the Victorian History of the County of Gloucestershire, Volume II
5.   Census of England and Wales Vol 1. HMSO London, 1912
6.   Census of England and Wales 1921 County of Gloucester, HMSO London, 1923
7.   Census of England and Wales 1931 County of Gloucester, Part I, HMSO London, 1933
8.   Census of England and Wales 1951 County Report, Gloucestershire, HMSO London, 1954
9.   Census of England and Wales 1961 County Report, Gloucestershire, HMSO London, 1964
10.   Census of England and Wales 1971 County Report, Gloucestershire, HMSO London, 1973
11.   Census 1981. OPCS Monitor. Ward and Civil Parish Monitor, Gloucestershire, 1984
12.   Census 1991 OPCS Monitor. Ward and Civil Parish Monitor, Gloucestershire, 1993 (obtained via the National Statistics website: www.statistics.gov.uk)
13.   Census 2001, obtained on line via www.ons.gov.uk/census/get-data/index.html
14.   Census of 1851 accessed through AncestryLibrary.com

All Census data are Crown copyright material which is reproduced with the permission of the Controller of HMSO.

Chapter 1.
THE HISTORY OF DIDBROOK SCHOOL

When the voices of children are heard on the green
And laughing is heard on the hill.

William Blake (1757-1827), Nurses Song

The early days

It is not known precisely when the first school was opened in Didbrook. However, the Parochial Returns of 1818 made to the Select Committee appointed by Parliament to inquire about the Education of the Poor included a statement for the 'consolidated parishes of Didbrooke, Hayles and Pinnock' by the Rector, John Eddy, as follows: 'No endowments for education of youth. Two small day schools, one consisting of 15 children, the other of 5; and a Sunday school, containing 61, supported by voluntary contributions. The poor have sufficient means of education' [1]. A similar report by CW Keysall, curate of Stanway reads: 'No endowments for the education of youth. A school consisting of 12 children, supported by the right hon dowager lady Elcho, open to the children of Taddington, a hamlet of Stanway and Cutterdean, in Worcestershire. The poorer class have sufficient means of education' and 'Another school, containing 19 children, of whom 10 are also paid for by the dowager lady Elcho' [1].

Thus, by the early 19th century there were two small day schools in Didbrook and Hailes (or Pinnock) and a Sunday School, and also two day schools in Stanway Parish, at Stanway and Taddington.

Until 1870 Didbrook's school is believed to have been situated in what is now the dining room of the blacksmith's cottage. Mrs Doreen Nurden, a grandchild of Wallace Jones, who was the blacksmith from 1913 until 1964, has confirmed this rumour. When Doreen was a child, her grandmother, Mrs Lizzie Jones (née Envine, born at Stanway around 1885) once told her this. The Envines had lived in Stanway for several generations so would have known the smithy and school well. The school bell was said to have been in the forge and there remains a bell housing high in the roof timbers; the bell is no longer present.

Calotype of the smithy at Didbrook circa 1860, probably taken by Lady Louisa Charteris, youngest daughter of Francis, 9th Earl of Wemyss. The blacksmith's house, the kitchen of which was used as a schoolroom, is obscured by a thatched cottage, which has since been lost (provided for publication by James, 13th Earl of Wemyss)

*Didbrook's smithy and the blacksmith's house
(photograph taken by JRM October 2004).*

*Bell housing of the school bell, situated in the roof of the smithy
(JRM, August 11th, 2009).*

Census records reveal that in 1851 Mrs Ann Harrison, aged 35 years, a widow born in Monmouthshire, was living and working as a school mistress in Didbrook; she was still in the post in 1861 (although was then recorded to have been born in Hereford). Another, presumably retired, school mistress, Mrs Hannah Martin, aged 66 years, was also recorded as living in the village in 1851; she had been born in Pinnock. By 1871 the school mistress lodging in Didbrook was Miss Kate Miller, who had been born in Bath [2]. Kelly's Post Office Directory of 1870 confirmed that Didbrook had 'a school, supported by voluntary subscriptions' and that Miss Miller was the school mistress; there were 'also a day and Sunday school at Hailes'. The Directory of 1874 recorded that Miss Mary Frost was then the school mistress, and the 1879 edition stated that Mrs Mary Alcock was the mistress and the school had been 'built in 1870' and was 'supported in part by Lord Sudeley' [3].

The main part of the present school, constructed of Cotswold stone, was built by the 3rd Baron Sudeley. A map of Didbrook dated 1848 [4] shows a cottage and a large garden on the site, whereas the Ordnance Survey map of 1884 [5] shows the school and its outhouses, which look like a pair of semi-detached houses, with a symmetrical pair of buildings and a pair of gardens or yards behind (see illustration). The school was built with a school house for the teacher at the Stanway end, and the school room at the Church end. It is unclear whether the original cottage was enlarged to provide this building, or whether it was demolished and the school and school house were built de novo. However, the former seems more likely, as judged by certain architectural features of the building which were revealed during renovations made in 2001/2, when evidence of lathe and plaster construction, fireplaces and chimneys in bedrooms and an old staircase were seen.

The development of the School

The School was placed under Government inspection in 1879, probably when Mrs Mary Alcock, Certificated Teacher, became the School Mistress on October 6th 1879. At that time Didbrook was part of the Toddington Estate, by then owned by the 4th Baron Sudeley (the 3rd Baron had died in 1877), and it was known as Didbrook Mixed School. The first surviving log book [6] was written by Mrs Alcock and she described how the school's work was overseen by Lord Sudeley's Stewards and the local clergy, Rev WD Stanton, Vicar of Toddington, and Rev J Fountain, Curate at Didbrook.

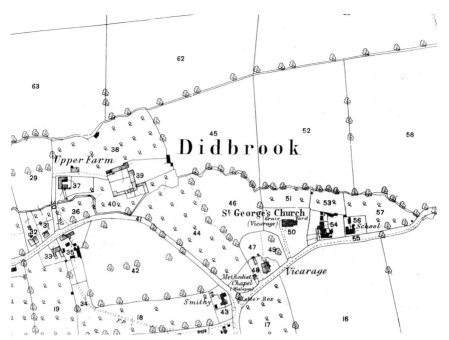

Detail showing Didbrook in an Ordnance Survey map of Stanway Parish, Crown copyright 1884, provided for publication by Gloucestershire Archives.

Didbrook.

Didbrook School, St George's Church and between them cottages, some time before 1921, when the school was altered.

Mrs Mary Alcock in middle age, seated, holding an open book (photograph provided by her grandson, Mr Bryan Markwell).

Mrs Alcock described the school as 'Didbrook Mixed School' and it was run as a Church School. Pupils were accepted from as young as 3 and normally left by the age of 13 years. Parents were charged fees for their children's education.

Mrs Alcock and one of her daughters and their pupils, circa 1910-1915
(photograph provided by Mr Glyn Wright).

Over the years the school had several changes of name, reflecting various changes in education, such as the school's amalgamation with Stanway School in 1921 and the opening of a Secondary Modern School at Winchcombe in 1952.

From its earliest years the school served a large area. Pupils came from Didbrook, Hailes, Hailes Hill, Ireley, Farmcote, Lynes Barn, Coscombe, Stumps Cross, Cutsdean, Taddington, Stanway and Toddington and sometimes further afield (even though some of these villages also had schools and the children had to walk to school). During the 20th century the schools in several neighbouring villages, including Stanway, Stanton and Laverton, closed and many of their pupils transferred to Didbrook.

In 1890, as a result of an exchange of land between the Stanway and Toddington Estates, Didbrook, including its school, became a part of Stanway Estate [7]. The Wemyss family, initially Hugo, Lord Elcho, then took over the role previously held by Lord Sudeley in respect to the School. The 1898/9 Returns of Schools and Accounts stated that it was a mixed, church school with accommodation for 81 pupils and an average attendance of 35. Under the Education Act of 1902 and a lease dated March 19th 1903 the yearly rent paid to the school's owner, the 10th Earl of Wemyss and March (Lord Elcho's father), was 2 shillings and 6 pence [8].

The average numbers of pupils at the school over nearly two centuries are shown in the figure. In the 19th century the figures recorded were usually average attendances and subsequently they were generally the average numbers of children on the school roll. During the 19th century the numbers were usually in the 30s or 40s and Mrs Alcock was the only teacher. However, in 1903 many children came into the area with the workers building the new railway line and were housed in huts near Toddington Station. The number of children at Didbrook School suddenly increased to 77 and reached nearly 100 by the end of the year. An Assistant Teacher was appointed to work with Mrs Alcock, and the number of monitors was increased. The children of the railway workers moved on with their families as the work was completed and had all left the school by March 1905, but school numbers remained in the 40s and 50s for several years and Mrs Alcock continued to have an Assistant until she retired at the age of 65 at the end of 1915.

Amalgamation of Didbrook and Stanway Schools

Due to falling school rolls and the cost of maintaining two schools within the Parish of Stanway, and the desire of the temporary head of Didbrook School, Miss Alcock, to leave her post, discussions were held in 1921 between the Elementary Schools Management sub-committee, the managers of Stanway C of E School and the Earl of Wemyss. It was agreed that Stanway children would go to Didbrook School, that Lord Wemyss would lease Didbrook School's Premises to the Education Committee, and that the Authority would bear the cost of enlarging the school building. Therefore, on June 1st 1921 Stanway School was closed and the children were transferred to Didbrook School, making a total of 56 pupils, 30 from Didbrook School and 26 from Stanway School. Miss Beatrice E Prothero, the head mistress of Stanway School, then became the head of the combined school at Didbrook. On August 30th, after the summer holiday, the school reopened as Didbrook Council School with Mr John Maybury as Head Teacher and Miss Maud Last as Supplementary Teacher.

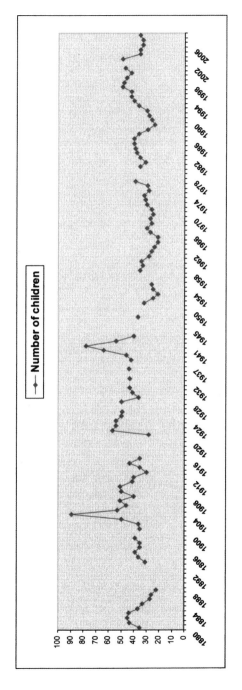

Figure showing the average numbers of children at Didbrook School from 1880 to 2008.

During the summer holidays and autumn term of 1922 alterations were made to Didbrook School, so until they were finished the pupils were taught in the building which had previously been Stanway School. The work involved incorporating the school house into the school, thereby providing one much larger classroom. This was subsequently divided by a screen to separate the infants from the older children. Thereafter teaching staff no longer lived in the school.

Mr Maybury left the school in 1922 and was replaced as head by Mr Cedric Stagg and a year later by Mr Lindsey Gay, who stayed until 1929. He was succeeded by Mrs Ada Holdsworth. She was the headmistress for 38 years and during them exerted a major influence on the development of the school.

The Second World War

War broke out with Germany in September 3rd 1939. On April 4th 1940 the first group of evacuees were received in the village and these were followed by others over the next 4½ years. They came from Bexhill, Birmingham, Dagenham, Eastbourne, Essex, Liverpool, London, Ramsgate and Worthing. At least 70 children were of school age and they attended Didbrook School. An extra teacher was recruited to assist the then Head Teacher, Mrs Holdsworth and Miss Last, the Infants Teacher, and the Wemyss Memorial (Village) Hall at Stanway became an extra classroom. The school roll increased to 78 for a time, but fell during the course of the war so that by early 1944 most of the evacuees had returned to their homes [9, 10] and pupil numbers became similar to those before the war.

On February 12th 1942 Miss Waghorne from Shire Hall called to discuss plans for school dinners and on April 13th, at the suggestion of the Education Authority, a School Canteen was opened within the school building. Mrs Brewin was appointed cook and, of 53 children on the roll, 40 had dinner. A charge of 1s-3d per week for infants and 1s-6d per week for older children was made. Miss Waghorne called to see the working of the canteen, stayed for dinner and expressed satisfaction at the organisation of the canteen and the evident enjoyment of the 43 children, out of 54 on the roll. In May 1944 Mrs Brewin left, so dinners were then supplied by Tewkesbury Feeding Centre until, in 1945, a purpose built canteen, built in the School grounds, was opened. The children were then provided with hot dinners cooked on the premises each day. Mrs Wright became the Canteen Cook.

The infant class in 1922, following the amalgamation of Stanway and Didbrook Schools, with their teacher, Miss Maud Last. Marjorie Archer, Jessica Edwards and Olga Jones are seated in the back row, 4th, 5th and 6th from the left (photograph provided by Mrs Wendy Butler, née Sadler).

The older children in 1922, with their teachers. Gladys Jones is seated in the middle row, 7th from the left (photograph provided by Mrs Wendy Butler).

Mrs Ada Holdsworth, head teacher 1929 to 1957, taken in Leeds before she came to Didbrook School (photograph provided by Mrs Joyce Stevens).

SCHOLASTIC SOUVENIR CO. LTD., BLACKPOOL.

Pupils at Didbrook School in 1935:

Front (1st) row: *Geoffrey Righton (?), unknown, unknown, Alf Buggins, Ron Nightingale*

2nd row: *Kathleen Stanford, (?) Wilkins, (?) Cox, unknown, John Cox, Cyril Gregory, Joyce Simpson, unknown, Nancy Simpson, unknown*

3rd row: *Cissy Parker, Betty Wright, unknown, Eric Doughty, Winnie Nightingale, unknown, unknown, Irene Doughty, unknown, Peggy Cox (?), Winnie Cox, Marjorie Doughty*

4th row: *Martin Innes, Barbara Lane, unknown, David Parker, Leslie Doughty, Betty Ingles, unknown, unknown, Mary Doughty, Molly Wright*

5th row: *Eva Cox, unknown, Peter Stanford, unknown, Hubert Wyniatt, (?) Doughty, unknown*

(photograph provided by Mrs Sandra Harris).

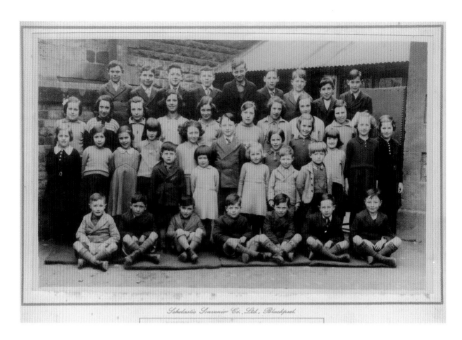

Pupils at Didbrook School in early 1939:

Front (1st) row: *Harry Turner, Douglas Vellender, unknown, Kenny Ingles, (?) Eric Righton, Roy Nightingale, John Cox*

2nd row: *Maurice Fletcher, Sheila Nightingale, Stella Baker, Tony Vellender, John Innes*

3rd row: *Joyce Simpson, Joan Vellender, unknown, Barbara Fletcher, June Gurton, Ron Nightingale, Barbara Hunt, Marjorie Righton, Rose Fletcher, Renee Baker, Nancy Simpson*

4th row: *Betty Wright, Marjorie Doughty, unknown, Joyce Fletcher, Peggy Ingles, Cissy Parker, Irene Doughty, Winnie Nightingale, unknown*

5th row: *Ronald Lane, Norman Cook, Alfie Buggins, Tom Fletcher, unknown, Eric Bolton, Harold Righton, unknown, Bill Nightingale*

(photograph provided by Mrs Sandra Harris).

Pupils at Didbrook School in October 1950:

Front (1st) row,
left to right: Eric Cook, Doreen Nightingale, Mary Knight, Tom Knight, Aileen and Wendy Jenkins, Margaret Hardiman, Janet Vellender, David and Joy Gregory, Richard Sadler

2nd row: Julie Beard, unknown, Billy Fathers, Susan and Margaret Mann, Brian Vellender, Patrick Newman, Pauline Whitcombe, Ann Sadler, Marian Vellender, Florence Wakefield, Eileen Vellender

3rd row: Sheila Stone, Peter Knight, ?Wakefield, Ann Holmes, Margaret Ingles, Marilyn Whitcombe, Elizabeth Holmes, Jean Nightingale, TonyGregory, Joel Roberts, Royston Nightingale, Robert Gregory

(photograph provided by Mrs Marian Roberts, née Vellender).

Aerial photograph showing the School,
the new canteen and the toilet block.

The School becomes a Primary School

Implementation of the Education Acts of 1944 and 1948 [11, 12], which separated primary and secondary education, resulted in the opening in January 1952 of Winchcombe Secondary Modern School. All the children aged 11 years or older were transferred there, reducing the roll at Didbrook School from 39 to 25 pupils. The roll then declined further and by January 1954 it was only 21, so the Education Authority transferred Miss Last to Toddington School; she transferred back in 1955, when the roll had risen again. The closure of Stanton School in the 1960s and of Laverton School in 1977 benefited Didbrook School; 11 Laverton pupils transferred to Didbrook, increasing its roll to 39. A new kitchen was built, as the canteen needed to be demolished, and in 1977 a prefabricated building (the 'terrapin') to provide a classroom to relieve overcrowding in the main building was also erected.

Over the years many of the school's sporting activities involved walking to Stanway, to use the cricket field there. However, in the early 1980s the Head, David Sanders, obtained permission from Mr Idiens of Hailes to use a field near the Salter's Way cottages for football. Then, in 1987, following discussions initiated by Catherine, Lady Neidpath (who was then a school governor) part of the old allotments area in Didbrook, across the road from the school, was fenced off to provide a football and sports field.   Lord Neidpath performed the opening ceremony on July 10th 1987 at the annual Sports Day. He made the field available for this purpose at no charge to the school and it has been well used.

The fight for survival

School rolls remained in the 30s and 40s for most of the 1970s and 1980s. However, for no particular reason it fell to the low 20s in 1989/90. This was particularly inopportune, as it coincided with the implementation of three new Government initiatives. These were the Education Reform Act 1988 [13], the Local Management of Schools (LMS) and the introduction of a National Curriculum.

Prior to LMS, schools were delegated money only for the day-to-day consumables, such as exercise books, stationery and art materials, at Didbrook around £250 per annum. All the other costs for staffing, power, building maintenance etc were funded centrally by the LEA, and the LEA decided what the teaching ratio would be. A small school like Didbrook was allowed to have 2.2 members of staff. So the current Head Teacher, David Sanders, and the Infants Teacher, Mrs Freeman were the only full-time staff, whilst a part-timer (0.2) could be employed for 1 day a week to allow the head teacher time for administration.

The LMS was a new mechanism for financing schools whereby all costs were delegated to the school. The governors (usually on the recommendation of the head teacher) allocated its budget as they considered appropriate.   Implementation of LMS and the National Curriculum, and other government directives, greatly increased the work of the teaching staff, and created extra financial costs. So it was not long before the cost per head of educating children was being calculated by the LEA. Rural schools appeared expensive because of the small number of their pupils, and economies were requested.

Nevertheless, it came as a shock when on May 20th 1991 the Chairman of the Governors, Charles Dickins, and the headmaster David Sanders, were invited to meet the County Education Sub-Committee at Shire Hall. They were asked to state their case for keeping the school open. Later that evening they were told that Didbrook was one of four schools that the Sub-Committee was recommending for closure. This decision was clearly being made for financial rather than educational reasons. A major campaign, involving the newspapers, radio and TV, was mounted by the staff, parents and governors. This was led by David Sanders, Charles Dickins and Lord Neidpath and the decision was reversed, mainly on the grounds that the children could not be offered the same type of (rural) education at Winchcombe that they were getting at Didbrook. Subsequently, Didbrook School's rolls increased to the 30s by 1993, to the 40s by 1994 and to the 50s by 1997.

In 1997 there was a review of Primary School Provision in the Winchcombe Area which posed another threat to the existence of both Didbrook and Toddington Schools. Many discussions were held and various options were considered, following which in 2000 the Secretary of State turned down the LEA's proposal to build an amalgamated school at Didbrook. However, money was made available to improve the building of the existing school at Didbrook, and Toddington School also remained open.

So that the work could be done on Didbrook School, from September 2001 to April 2002 the pupils and teachers moved to the former Winchcombe Primary School in Back Lane in Winchcombe. The work was completed in two stages. During the two terms that the pupils were taught in Winchcombe, the terrapin was demolished, two new classrooms were built on the north side of the school, a small library was created and the toilets were incorporated within the building, whereas previously they had been separate from it.

Once the pupils were back at Didbrook, the second phase was undertaken which comprised the total renovation of the 'Victorian' building to provide a hall/internal games area, with upgrading of the electrical services and provision of a sports floor. A small room was created above the staffroom, with access via a fixed staircase from the end of the hall. The total cost of the project was

Mrs Alison Whiston,
Chairman of the Governors,
helping with the move to
Winchcombe,
September 2001.

Children and their teacher, Mrs Sue Brewin, in a classroom at Winchcombe, 2001.

The school garden, with vegetable patch, greenhouse and pond, 2008 (JRM).

around £300,000 and much credit is due to Mrs Alison Whiston, Chairman of the Governors then, for her work on leading this remodelling of the School. The official opening of the new premises was conducted by Lord Neidpath and David Sanders on July 16th 2003, and the refurbishment was completed in October 2003.

Another innovation, to provide a school garden, occurred in 2002, following Lord Neidpath's gift to the school of part of the adjacent cottage's allotment. In June 2004 a pond was added and in June 2005 a greenhouse. The driving force behind this development was a parent, later a Governor, Gaynor Edwards. As well as enhancing the environs of the school, the new garden and pond also provided a valuable additional teaching area, where pupils study plants and insects and other living creatures, to add to their education, particularly in science and art.

In 2005 the County Council Review Panel reassessed all its schools and recommended that Didbrook and Toddington Schools should close in 2008. This news was received with amazement at Didbrook School, so soon after such a major upgrade of its facilities. At that time its roll was about 34. Negotiations then took place which culminated in an agreement in September 2006 that Didbrook and Toddington Schools would amalgamate in September 2008.

A Temporary Governing Body was set up and the members agreed that the new School would operate from the sites of both Didbrook and Toddington Schools. They appointed Mrs Lesley Marriott (Head of Toddington School) to become the Head of the new School from September 2008. Then, following the appointment of the Head of Didbrook School, Mr David Ogden, to the Headship of Temple Guiting School, Mrs Marriott became Acting Head of Didbrook School, in January 2008.

A Service of Thanksgiving for the Life of Didbrook School was held at St George's Church, Didbrook, on July 17th, 2008, when it closed at the end of the summer term. The church was packed with pupils past and present, parents, teachers, governors and other friends and supporters of the school. Each child was given a flower pot containing soil and a calendula flower seed to take home. After the service, everyone enjoyed a barbeque in the school grounds.

Didbrook School 2008. One of the new classrooms can be seen behind the school, jutting out to the right, (JRM).

Didbrook School 2008. One of the two new classrooms is seen to the right and also the subsequent improvements to the playground, (JRM).

SOURCES

1. Education of the Poor. A Digest of Parochial Returns made to the Select Committee appointed to inquire into the Education of the Poor, Session of 1818, Vol 1, ordered by the House of Commons, 1.4.1819, pages 321, 325 and 1464. Public Records Office, Kew.
2. Microfiche copies of Census records of 1851, 1861, 1871, 1881, held in Gloucestershire Archives
3. Kelly's Post Office Directories of 1870, 1874, 1879
4. Map of Didbrook, 1848, showing 'Apportionment of the rent charges in lieu of tithes', Gloucestershire Archives
5. Ordnance Survey map of Didbrook , 1884, held in Gloucestershire Archives
6. Log books of Didbrook School from October 6th, 1879 to March 25th 1993
7. James Charteris, 13th Earl of Wemyss
8. Tenure and Trusts of Voluntary Schools, list 32, HMSO London, Eyre and Spottiswoode, 1907
9. Admission Registers 1918 to 1982
10. Official evacuation list for Stanway Council School, Gloucestershire County Archives
11. Education Act (Butler) 1944
12. Education (Miscellaneous Provisions) Act 1948
13. Education Reform Act 1988

Other Sources

1. Head Teachers' Reports and Minutes of Governors' meetings 1991 to June 1st 2008
2. Elementary Schools Management sub committee minutes CE/M3/18, Gloucestershire Archives
3. Interview with Mr David Sanders
4. Interview with Mr David Ogden
5. Interview with Mrs Doreen Nurden

Chapter 2.
THE HISTORY OF STANWAY SCHOOL

The school has also been known as Stanway National School, Stanway
C. E. School, W County of Gloucester, No 3314 (June 1st 1893 or earlier)
and Stanway C of E School No 298 (1906 or earlier).

Train up a child in the way he should go: and when he is old, he
will not depart from it.

The Proverbs of Solomon XXIII, 6, The Holy Bible

The early days

A school was present in Stanway from at least as early as the late 18th
century, when there were two schoolteachers, one at Church Stanway
and one at Wood Stanway, each paid by the owner of the Stanway estate,
who was then Viscountess Hereford, a descendent of the Tracy family [1,
2]. By 1825 the day school at Stanway had 24 pupils [3] and in 1831 it was
said that the 8th Earl of Wemyss (who inherited the estate after Lady
Hereford's death in 1817) supported two schools there [4]. Another
source, however, suggests that the second school (in 1818 supported by
the Dowager Lady Elcho) was at Taddington [5]. The national Census of
1851 showed that by then there were two school mistresses living in
Stanway, Mrs Jane Weir (a widow aged 55 years) in Wood Stanway and
Mrs Martha Pritchard (a widow aged 70 years) in Church Stanway [6].

The precise location of the early schools on Stanway estate is unknown,
but in 1857 Stanway National School was opened in a stone building
belonging to the 9th Earl of Wemyss situated on the Tewkesbury to Stow
Road, just below Lidcombe Wood. The building had a schoolroom and
accommodation for the teacher. The school had an uncertificated
teacher paid by the Earl of Wemyss and was also supported by
endowments and school pence. The average daily attendance was 38
and there was an evening school on three evenings a week as well [7].
From 1858 the school received an annual grant from the Government [8].
The average attendance in 1878 was 36 [9] and by 1903 it had increased to
48 [10]. In 1902 the school was recorded to have accommodation for 66
children, average attendance 41, the building being owned by the 10th
Earl of Wemyss, but by then leased under Section 24 of the Education Act
(1902) to the Education Authority at an annual rent of £8 [11].

Most of the further information about Stanway School was derived from the two Log Books which were written by the successive Head Teachers, with occasional entries by the current vicar, HMI and Diocesan visitor [12].

Calotype of Stanway School circa 1860, probably taken by Lady Louisa Charteris, youngest daughter of Francis, 9th Earl of Wemyss. The thatched cottage in front of the school has since been replaced by a stone cottage (provided for publication by James, 13th Earl of Wemyss).

The development of the School

The first Log Book, started by the school mistress Miss Catherine Edwards, begins *'1863. March 9th. A short attendance in morning. Half holiday in afternoon to prepare for the festivities of the 10th'*. The festivities were not described. Her records include descriptions of the frequent visits paid to the school by the local vicar and school manager, Rev Francis R Traill. Like the clergy who oversaw the work of Didbrook School, Rev Traill and his successors checked the registers, summarised the reports made by HMIs, gave Religious instruction, and opened the school when the mistress was absent. Mrs Traill also helped, by teaching the children knitting, overseeing their sewing, presenting prizes etc. Rev Traill died in 1883 and his role was taken over by his successor, Rev RF Mallam (who was succeeded over the years by Revs SJ Walker, F Bullock-Webster, Collins Ashton, SE Cornish, Oscar Worne, Eustace Bateman and GN Bennett).

Lord Wemyss's agent, G Makepiece Esquire (and his successors, who included Mr CH Smith) paid occasional visits to the school, as did members of the Wemyss family and their friends. For example in October 1880, and also in some subsequent years, Lady Elcho brought books to be distributed among the children and in 1882 she provided prizes for pupils who had done good work. For a number of years Lord and Lady Elcho gave each child a '*Child's Almanack*' at Christmas. In August 1882 the children attended a '*treat*' at '*the Mansion*' (Stanway House) and a similar event was provided in 1883 to celebrate Lord Elcho's wedding. After this, each year Lord and Lady Elcho hosted a summer party at Stanway House for the children. In 1886 Lady Elcho provided three maps and a quantity of Scripture prints for the school, for use in lessons and to decorate the walls. In July 1887 Queen Victoria's Golden Jubilee was celebrated: '*The children gathered at the school and were decorated with medals and then walked to church with flags headed by Toddington Brass Band. After the service all were admitted into Lord Elcho's Grounds and were entertained with Dinner, tea, sports etc until late.*' From the early 1890s Lord and Lady Elcho or the vicar hosted a Christmas Tree event for the children and from time to time the successive vicars and their wives invited them to tea parties and games. In the 1900s the children who had done well at school were given prizes and medals, which Lady Elcho or the vicar would present.

Towards the end of the 19th century, at times when the school roll was high the accommodation for the children became cramped. Thus, in 1893 some children were being taught in the kitchen of the schoolhouse and in the lobby. Another problem was that during the winter months the schoolroom was very cold, recorded in the first week of January 1894 as between 34 and 44 degrees Fahrenheit, and as low as 28.1 in mid-January that year. Children had to go to the fire for warmth and many were away sick. Similar winter temperatures were recorded in subsequent years and in 1894 the HMI requested that the latticed window panes be replaced by plain glass to reduce draughts.

In 1907 the Log Book records difficulties arising from the Council refusing to pay for maintenance of the school building and wear and tear. In 1913 Miss Prothero drew attention to a number of defects in the building and its environs that needed to be remedied, including the danger for children from motor traffic when they were going to the '*conveniences*', which were some distance from the school gate. This danger had been manifest on October 25th 1909 when '*a terrible accident to two children occurred during the dinner hour. A van attached to a Traction Engine ran from the road on to the path and into the hedge where the children had retreated, the injuries to the little boy of 6 being fatal.'* The Log Books provide no evidence that the Council did anything to reduce these hazards.

Teaching Staff

During much of the 19th century most teachers were still uncertificated, including those teaching at Stanway School. The first teacher training college in Britain was opened in Battersea, London, in 1840 by Dr Kay (later Lord Kay-Shuttleworth) and by 1845 the Church of England had 22 training colleges [12]. The table lists all the teaching staff at Stanway School from 1863 until its amalgamation with Didbrook School in 1921. The Log Book indicates that, particularly in the 1860s and 1870s, there were difficulties in recruiting and retaining good teachers at Stanway and in 1866 the school had to close for five months because of the serious illness of the schoolmistress. The children's progress was impaired by these problems and in 1869, following the HMI's inspection, the government grant was reduced by 10% and the grant was deducted altogether *'for the three months during which the School was not under a Certificated Teacher'*. Moreover, while working as teachers at the school, some schoolmistresses were still studying for their certificates. Examples were Mrs Emilie Innes, who was awarded her certificate in July 1870, and Miss Isabella Smith, whose was awarded in 1882.

On August 12th 1869 Mr Makgill spoke to the Mistress, Mrs Innes, about a reduction of her salary, stating that the Managers were unable to meet the expenses of the School, because the average number of pupils had fallen as a result of so many schools being opened in surrounding districts. It is perhaps not surprising that soon after she received her certificate in 1870, Mrs Innes left, probably to a go to a better paid post.

There were no entries in the Log Book from July 1873 until January 1877, but the school appears to have remained open during this time, as attendance in 1877 averaged 40. There is a note that, following a change of teacher, the Log Book was again not completed from August 1878, until an inspection by Mr Bateman HMI on March 21st 1879, after which the record was resumed.

In 1879 Miss Isabella Smith became the schoolmistress and, though still uncertificated, was particularly effective. The HMIs report of January 1881 was summarised by Rev Traill thus: *'Stanway C of E School. Miss*

Smith has evidently taken great pains with the Discipline and the teaching of this little School, and the results of her work are far better than anything that Stanway School has produced for some years. The children are orderly. They read well, write very fairly, spell well, and are fairly taught in Arithmetic. In this Subject, the second standard and the boys of the first Standard did very well indeed. Of the eight who failed in this three were only just of age to be examined.' Despite these comments, in July 1881 the Vicar, Rev Traill, proposed that Miss Smith should in future be paid £35 per annum plus half of the annual Government Grant, reducing her annual salary by £15. Following an intervention by the Head Manager, Mr Randall, she received a note from Rev Traill suggesting that she should be paid £35 p.a. plus ¾ of the Government grant. She agreed on condition that she continued to be paid, in total, at her current salary of £60. However, in 1882, shortly after she received her certificate, Miss Smith moved to another post.

The first fully certificated teacher at Stanway School was probably Miss Mary Ross, who was appointed in 1892. The standard of work achieved by the children under her tutelage was highly praised by the HMI, Mr FB de Sausmarez, and in 1895 he awarded the highest grant to the school for every subject. Sadly for the school, in April 1995 Miss Ross left Stanway because she had been promoted to be Headmistress of the Rectory Park Girls School, Bishopswearmouth, (average attendance 413 pupils) at a minimum salary of £160 p.a., considerably more than a small school like Stanway could afford.

There is mention in the Log Books on a number of occasions from 1891 onwards of the presence of an Assistant teacher at the school, but there were still periods when the Headmistress was single-handed or working with the help of only a Monitress. On January 21st 1897 Mr de Sausmarez, HMI recorded *'This is an excellent school….. results of the examination very satisfactory indeed, but it is doubtful if any teacher working single-handed can maintain this high level. A Monitress should therefore be provided to look after the infants…..'* By October that year a monitress was in post and in 1898, when there were 52 children on the books, Miss Frost also started, as Assistant Mistress; she stayed until the school closed in 1921. However, in 1907, because of financial difficulties, Miss Frost's salary was reduced from £30 p.a. to that of a monitress (£10 p.a.) until November 1908, when it was increased to £15 p.a. and November 1910 when it became £25. She did not receive her full salary of £70 p.a. until her last year in post.

Table 3.
Teachers at Stanway School

Head Teachers

Miss Catherine Edwards	from March 1863 (or earlier) to December 31st, 1864
Miss Harriet Jones	from early 1865 to October 19th, 1865
Mr George Frederick Long	from March 26th, 1866 to August 16th, 1867
Ms Julia Hughes	from September 30th, 1867 to December 19th, 1867
Ms Emily Clara Fowler	from January 6th, 1868 to a date in 1869
Mrs Emilie Claretta Innes	from a date in 1869 to November 1970 or January 1871

[Note Ms Emily Fowler and Mrs Emilie Innes were probably the same person. Mrs Innes had a sister called Miss Fowler who stood in on November 27th 1970 when Mrs Innes was ill]

Ms Elizabeth Goodacre	from January 9th 1871 to ?February 4th 1872
Miss J Tennant	from February 5th 1872 to ?
Mrs Rosanna Hall	dates uncertain, included 1879
Miss Isabella J Smith	from July 21st, 1879 to October 27th 1882
Miss Emily Wright	from November 1st, 1882 to March 30th 1892
Miss Mary Ross	(certificated teacher) from April 4th 1892 to April 29th 1895
Miss Bessie Belbin	from September 2nd 1895 to October 21st 1897
Miss Beatrice Ellen Prothero	from January 31st 1898 to June 1st 1921 (when she moved, with her Stanway School pupils, to Didbrook School on their amalgamation. She then became head of the amalgamated school for a short time)
Mrs May Prothero	from February 10th to April 25th 1915 (while Miss BE Prothero was on sick leave)

Other Teachers

Miss Roberts	(teacher of drawing) from April 6th 1891 to ?
Mrs FA Wiggett	(Assistant Teacher) from November 9th 1891 to ?
Ms E Hopkins	(Assistant Teacher) from April 11th 1892 for a period, then for a further period as a temporary assistant, from October 1894 for about three months
Miss Eliza Ross	(Assistant Teacher, appointed under Article 68) from December 1st 1892 to ? August 1985
Miss Maria E Frost	(Assistant Mistress) from May 2nd 1898 to March 31st 1921
Miss Alcock	(Temporary Assistant) from April 19th to 25th 1917

Monitors

Iris Trinder	1864 or earlier to
Mary Lediard	from October 3rd, 1865 to ?
Jane Starkey	from May 13th 1878 to ?
Kate Price	from October 3rd 1889 to March 2nd 1890
Miss Lily Lane	from March 3rd 1890 to
Others	details unknown
Miss Minnie Stratford	from May 4th 1903 to about August 1903, during Miss Frost's illness
Miss Maud Last	(Temporary Monitress) for a few days from April 16th 1917, while Miss Frost was away

Generally, the HMI's reports indicated that good academic results were obtained at Stanway School, despite the staffing and financial problems there. On May 5th 1897 F Russell left, having won a scholarship to Winchcombe Grammar School and on May 8th 1919 Ernest and Alida Mockett left the school, having passed examinations to Pate's Grammar School, Cheltenham.

The War Years 1914-1918

The Log Book includes little about the impact of World War I on the school. In 1914 the girls knitted socks for the soldiers and in 1917 the children picked blackberries for them, for which they received 1d per pound. However, certain entries suggest that the number of men in the area serving or killed in the war was having a serious impact on the local community, particularly on farming. Thus, on February 11th 1918 five of the seven big boys were absent: '*Vellender and Bowles driving plough for farmers, Mockett with a headache, John Last not sent and Cyril Envine with ringworm*' and on May 9th '*Boys are continuously having days or half days to help with land*'. On June 28th Miss Prothero wrote '*Application from farmers to allow boys for haymaking. Have asked that school be closed for fortnight for this purpose*'. This was agreed. On August 5th '*Christopher Vellender returned after an absence of nearly 5 months*' and on August 13th '*Vellender absent again - gone to work*'. Also, although the school reopened after the summer holidays on September 16th the children went blackberry picking on 3 days that week.

The treaty of Versailles was signed to end WWI on June 28th 1919 and on June 30th the children celebrated this event in their lessons in History and Geography. Also, during July lessons were held on the reasons Great Britain entered the war and the countries and people involved. On July 15th the school closed for three days during which Peace celebrations, limited to the entertainment of children and soldiers, were held. Armistice Day was first commemorated at the school on November 11th 1919, when the vicar visited and two minutes silence was held.

Amalgamation of Stanway and Didbrook Schools

During WWI around 40 children were on the books of Stanway School, but in 1919 they fell to 38 and by 1921 to only 28. The Assistant Mistress, Miss Frost, retired on March 31st 1921 and was not replaced. The changes at Stanway coincided with a similar decline in pupil numbers at

Didbrook School, where the temporary supply teacher (Miss Mary Alcock) desired to be released from her post. So it was agreed that the two schools would be amalgamated at Didbrook under the headship of Miss Prothero (head of Stanway School) on June 1st 1921, and that Stanway School would close. All the pupils were taught in Stanway School for period in 1922, while alterations were made to Didbrook School, but after that the vacated Stanway School was used to house the head of Didbrook School.

SOURCES

1. Stanway memorandum bk. and acct.bk
2. Victoria County History, Volume VI, 1965, page 231-2
3. Gloucestershire Diocesan Records, vol.383
4. Lewis, Topog.Dict.Eng. (1831), iv. 107
5. Education of the poor. A Digest of Parochial Returns made to the Select Committee appointed to inquire into the Education of the Poor. Session of 1818. Volumes I, pages 289, 312 and 321 and III page 1464. Ordered by the House of Commons April 1st 1819
6. Census of 1851, accessed through AncestryLibrary.com.
7. Ministry of Education. Public Elementary Schools, Preliminary Statements 7/37
8. Rep.of Educ.Cttee.of Council, 1858 [2510], p.566, H.C. (1859 Sess. 1), xxi (1)
9. Ibid. 1878 [C.2342-I], p.896,HC (1878-9), xxiii
10. Public Elem.Schools, 1906 [Cd.3182] p189, HC. 1906, lxxxvi
11. Areas Subject to Local Education Authorities under Part III of Education Act 1902 for Gloucester County Borough Council, in Tenure and Trusts of Voluntary Schools. In: List 32. Schools in England and Wales recognised on January 1st 1906 as Voluntary Public Elementary Schools, showing the tenure of the premises and character of the Trusts, if any, to which premises subject. HMSO London, Eyre and Spottiswoode, 1907
12. The Log Books of Stanway School, Volume I March 9th 1863 to January 30th 1895 and Volume II February 1895 to May 31st, 1921. The latter was made available by Gloucestershire Archives (Reference S308/1).
13. Curtis SJ. History of Education in Great Britain, 7th Edition, University Tutorial Press, London, 1967.

Chapter 3.
TEACHERS AT DIDBROOK SCHOOL

Those that do teach young babes
Do it with gentle means and easy tasks.
William Shakespeare (1564-1616). Othello, Act IV, Sc i.

Full many a flower is born to blush unseen,
And waste its sweetness on the desert air.
Thomas Gray (1716-1771). Elegy in a Country Churchyard

Little is known of earlier teaching staff, but there is a good record of the many teachers who have taught at Didbrook School since its present building opened in the 1870s (see the table). Three had a particularly large influence on the school, Mrs Alcock, Mrs Holdsworth and Mr Sanders, who between them held the post of Head Teacher for 98 years. Miss Last, who was a pupil, a monitor and then for 42 years, the infant teacher, also made an enormous contribution to the life of the school. Details of their lives and work, and vignettes of some of the other Head Teachers who gave so much to the school follow.

Mrs Mary Drury Alcock (head for 36 years, from 1879 to 1915)

Mrs Alcock was born on December 15th 1850 to Samuel Drury of Chipping Campden and his second wife, Grace Slade, one of seven children of the family. A priest there recognised Mary's abilities and suggested that she should go to Hockerill College, Bishop's Stortford, in Hertfordshire to train as a teacher. She was admitted when she was 17 years old and duly gained her teaching certificate. She worked as a teacher thereafter, without respite, until she reached the retirement age of 65 years, despite marrying and having a large family of her own [1, 2]. According to her grandson, Bryan Markwell, her favourite quotation was from Gray's Elegy, shown above.

Family tradition has it that Mary's future husband, Alfred Alcock, first saw her when he galloped his horse past her pony and trap in a field at Temple Guiting. It was 'love at first sight' and he decided there and then that he would marry her. Alfred was born at Temple Guiting circa 1852 and later lived at Hawling Manor with his parents and 8 brothers and sisters. Mary and Alfred married in Gloucester Register Office on December 1st 1873. Some time later they lived at Temple Guiting Manor, a property which belonged to the Diocese of Oxford and where, in 1878, their 3rd child was born.

The following year, Mary was appointed Mistress of Didbrook Mixed School so she, her husband Alfred and their children Alfred Harry, Charles and Adelina Mary moved to the village. At first they lived in the school house, but later, as their family grew, they moved to a cottage adjacent to the School, next door to the Archer family.

Altogether the Alcocks had fourteen children. Eleven of Mary's children were born at Didbrook and it is remarkable that she continued teaching throughout these pregnancies. Five confinements were during school holidays (which in at least two instances appear to have been scheduled to suit her needs). Mary's duties were undertaken by another teacher for five weeks in 1884, probably after Alfred's birth, while for the confinements of the remaining five children born at Didbrook, teachers from elsewhere took over for periods of two or three weeks *during the illness of the mistress*.

Mrs Mary Alcock and her husband, Alfred, standing by a convertible car with the hood down outside Didbrook School, circa 1910-15.
Seated in the car are their four youngest daughters, Charlotte, Bessie, Jenny and Gwendoline and three men friends (photograph provided by their great grand-daughter, Mrs Elisabeth Brett).

Mary's husband Alfred was an engineer and worked as a supplier of agricultural equipment. He was also a talented pianist and organist and played the organ at Sudeley for many years.

Tragically, three of Mary and Alfred's offspring died young, John died in infancy and Edith Adelaide of typhoid fever in 1904 at the age of 23 years. Edith was a talented singer, 'the Nightingale of Gloucestershire', and had just started her career as an opera singer. It is said that her sister, Grace, kissed her in Didbrook church at the funeral and caught typhoid from her, but fortunately survived. Their brother, Alfred, who was a Second Lieutenant in the 1st Battalion, Gloucestershire Regiment, died in 1916 in the Battle of the Somme. Mary and Alfred's grandson, Oswald Culverwell, was also killed in action, over Berlin during WW II. However, many of Mary and Alfred's descendants had distinguished careers in the United Kingdom or Australia, including two grandsons who became consultant dental surgeons, another who was Minister of Transport in Tasmania and a great grandson who became a barrister [1,2,3].

Mrs Mary Alcock and Bessie, both in mourning dress after the death of Edith in 1901 (photograph provided by Mrs Elisabeth Brett).

Mrs Alcock worked single-handedly as the Mistress of Didbrook School for the first 24 of the 36 years that she spent teaching there. She was assisted by only a monitor until Miss Florence Stanford joined her as Assistant Teacher in 1903. Mary implemented the various educational changes brought about by successive governments and her school was awarded government grants. Horace Holmes (born in 1909) remembered Mrs Alcock well. She was headmistress when he started at the school and he said that she was a very nice person, much liked by her pupils [4]. He recollected an escapade when he was playing with the author's father in the playground. They were not allowed out of the playground during breaks, but my father wanted to play in the neighbouring field. So, when he thought that no-one was looking, my father jumped over the hedge into the field and Horace tried to follow. However, Horace got stuck on top and hurt himself slightly and had to be helped down. All this had been watched through the window by Mrs Alcock, who called the boys in and caned them lightly on the hands. Horace said that he was caned first and it was not at all painful. However, when Dad was caned, he grasped the cane and ran away with it and threw it down the lavatory!

As well as being a successful Headmistress of the school, Mary also became a much respected and influential member of the community. She was compassionate and at least twice gave evidence in court at Winchcombe in support of former pupils. One was a lad with learning difficulties who had behaved inappropriately in the village street and the other was a girl accused of concealing an illegitimate pregnancy; both were acquitted. Also, despite the size of her large family and her teaching commitments, when the parents of one of her grandchildren separated, Mary had her little grandson, Oswald Culverwell, to live with her for several years. Tragically, Oswald was killed in action over Berlin on June 22nd 1944, when serving with the RAF Volunteer Reserve.

In middle age Mary had an infection of her right eye, which had to be removed, and in later photographs she is seen wearing a patch over the socket.

Mary retired on December 31st 1915, at the age of 65 years, but remained a school manager for some years afterwards. She lived to the great age of 94 years, and was buried in Didbrook Churchyard on March 23rd, 1945. Hers was the last funeral at Didbrook at which Rev HB Allen officiated.

Alfred Alcock died on October 17th 1927 aged 74 years and was also buried in Didbrook Churchyard, on October 19th.

Their daughters Mary, Lottie and Bessie were monitors at Didbrook School, and Mary, Lottie, Jennie, and Bessie all spent short periods as temporary or assistant teachers there.

Mrs Ada Alice Holdsworth (head for 38 years, from 1929 to 1957)

Mrs Holdsworth (née Slater, born March 13th 1898, died aged 80 years in 1978) was a Yorkshire woman who reputedly was offered the headship of Didbrook School and a school in London at the same time. Fortunately she decided to work at Didbrook, possibly choosing a country school because of her husband's health - Colin (born Louis Colin Holdsworth on June 25th 1891 and married to Ada in Leeds in 1926) was gassed in WW I and was diabetic, so could not do heavy work. However, Colin cultivated a good garden, kept bees and became one of several local barbers.

When in 1929 Mrs Holdsworth arrived alone at Toddington Station, my father, who had been sent to meet her, was greeted by a formidable lady carrying one large heavy suitcase and her Singer sewing machine. He took her to her temporary lodgings in Wood Stanway and Colin joined her later. They lived at Hill Stanway in the old School House until Colin's death in 1969, after which Mrs Holdsworth moved to a cottage at Hill Stanway, just above the old post office and telephone box.

Energetic and of high principles and robust health, Mrs Holdsworth (affectionately known as 'Granny Holdsworth' although she had no children of her own) went everywhere on her bicycle, which had a basket in front of the handlebars and a wooden box behind the seat for her books and papers. She was a disciplinarian, but fair and greatly respected by her pupils and their parents. Corporal punishment was accepted then, but not often administered - caning on the hand or use of the slipper to the clothed 'bottom'. She always wanted the best for her pupils and took great pride in their achievements, but was intolerant of sloth. By 1944, when I first met her, her straight hair, which was parted in the middle, then plaited and twisted in a bun at the nape of her neck, was greying. She wore no make-up and 'sensible' flat shoes. She taught all subjects, the three R's, but also literature, poetry, elocution, sewing, knitting, natural history (she lead occasional 'nature walks' around the country lanes), scripture, PE, singing, country dance and much more.

Mrs Ada Holdsworth outside the cottage on Stanway Hill where she lived after Colin's death (photograph provided by Mrs J Stevens).

No one could leave the school without a comprehensive knowledge of the hymn book and of English folk songs, such as 'Early one morning', 'Drink to me only', 'Afton water' and ' The Lincolnshire poacher'- the last sung with perhaps more than necessary vigour by some of the older boys. She also taught country dancing to the music of her wind-up gramophone- 'Strip the willow', the 'Barn dance' and 'Roger de Coverley'. Mrs Holdsworth led by example and admonished her pupils with many sayings: 'If a thing's worth doing it's worth doing well', 'A stitch in time saves nine', 'A rolling stone gathers no moss'......... She also gave sound practical advice. For example, Margaret Varnish (née Mann) remembers being told 'always take a clean handkerchief when you go for an interview', and she did exactly that on every occasion, with success!

As well as the broad syllabus undertaken within the school, Mrs Holdsworth organised many educational excursions, paid for from funds raised at school concerts and other events. These included visits to Bristol Zoo and Fry's chocolate factory, the Three Counties Show, Gloucester Cathedral, Shakespeare's plays at Stratford Memorial Theatre, Cheltenham Art Gallery and Museum, and Hailes Abbey and Church.

In 1938 she and Miss Last took 8 senior children on an educational visit to London for a week. A summary of the costs of this visit is interleaved in the school's Log Book. The expenditure on insurance, fares, hotel accommodation, meals, admission fees, medicine, first aid and tips came to £21-16s-11½d (£2-14s-7½d per child) and was paid for from the savings of the 8 children (£1 each), a rummage sale, and the School Fund; the deficit (15s-10½d) was paid by Mrs Holdsworth herself. One incident recounted about the trip concerned their last day, when the children were allowed half an hour near Trafalgar Square to buy presents to take back for their parents. Mrs Holdsworth noticed that the present in a paper bag held by one pupil, Lancelot Jones, appeared to be moving. She asked to see it and found that there was a live pigeon in the bag. Lancelot explained that he wanted it to breed with his pigeon at home. She insisted that it be released. Unfortunately these visits ceased with the onset of the Second World War in 1939.

Mrs Holdsworth was strongly patriotic and on Empire Day the children and teachers gathered around the school's flagpole, flying the Union Flag, for morning service which ended with the National Anthem. When George V died she held a special service at the school and gave a talk to the children about his reign. She also arranged for them to listen to the radio broadcast of the Proclamation of the Accession of Edward VIII. She subsequently gave special lessons on the Coronation of George VI. On August 10th 1944 Mrs Holdsworth discovered that Queen Mary was going to travel along the road from Winchcombe to Broadway. She got one of the bigger boys to carry the Union Flag and the whole school hurried in a long crocodile behind him to Hailes turn. We arrived just in time to see a smart black car pass by with the upright figure of the Queen in a pale silk dress and a matching toque hat, sitting in the back.

During the war years Mrs Holdsworth assisted with the placement of many evacuees in homes in the villages and arranged for an extra classroom to be opened in the Wemyss Memorial Hall to accommodate 27 senior pupils and relieve overcrowding in the school. She visited the schools in Birmingham from which many of the evacuees came, to liaise with their teachers there.

With the end of hostilities in 1945 came expectations of a more varied and luxurious way of life, but rationing of food, clothing and petrol and other difficulties continued for several more years.

Nevertheless, in 1946 Mrs Holdsworth arranged the first cricket match against another school, Stanton, which was played on Stanway Cricket Ground. Glyn Wright remembers playing and that the other members of the Didbrook School team included Douglas and Tony Vellender, Kenny Ingles and Ron Nightingale. Didbrook won, but lost their next match against Winchcombe School.

Mrs Holdsworth also wanted to obtain better facilities in the school and to resume educational school trips, so she organised fundraising concerts and other events to provide for these. In 1950 she held a jumble sale in aid of the Lord Mayor of London's Thank-offering fund: families gave generously and the older pupils, including the author, assisted Mrs Holdsworth and Miss Last in pricing the items and manning tables on which they were displayed. Half an hour before the sale was due to start a long queue of eager women stretched down the road almost to the blacksmith's. At 2 pm the doors were opened and there was a frenzy of bargaining and buying, with nearly all items sold, even decrepit clothing. When the money was counted there was so much that, as well as making a donation to the Lord Mayor's Fund, Mrs Holdsworth and Miss Last were able to take a party of 21 older pupils to London for the day.

We went to London by bus to Moreton-in-Marsh and then by train to Paddington and had a wonderful day, seeing the Changing of the Guard at Buckingham Palace, Trafalgar Square and many other sights. I particularly remember the Tower of London and being fascinated by all the armour and weapons. One of the warders decided to give Miss Last amd me a personal conducted tour, at the end of which Miss Last tipped him a shilling- so I gave him my threepenny bit. When we emerged into the sunlight outside, we were roundly told off by Mrs Holdsworth for keeping everyone waiting.

Mrs Holdsworth took an active part in village life, was an enthusiastic member of the Women's Institute and she helped organise the annual Stanway Flower Show and Fete for many years. A regular churchgoer, she sat in the same pew every week about half way up the right side of the aisle, with Miss Last, the infant teacher, as befitted her station, sitting in the pew behind her. She also supported the Trade Union movement and was an active member of the National Union of Teachers. She represented the County NUT at the Women's Voluntary Service's Meetings at Gloucester.

After she retired in 1957 Mrs Holdsworth remained active with voluntary work in the Parish, including organising a chiropody clinic for the elderly at the Wemyss Memorial Hall. She also took a number of overseas holidays. She died at home in her cottage in 1978 after a short illness.

Miss Maud Alice Flora Last
(pupil, then monitor 1917 to 1921 and infant teacher 1921 to 1963)

Maud (born circa 1903, baptised June 7th 1903, died aged 87 years on January 9th 1990, ashes interred January 21st 1991) was one of the children of John (Jack) Last, Head Gamekeeper on Stanway Estate, and his wife, Clara Louise. They lived in the house to the west of Stanway Churchyard, which is close to Stanway Cricket Ground where Maud enjoyed watching matches. Maud had a sister, Gladys, who went to live in York after she married Roy Bovill. She also had a brother Jack (John?) who visited her occasionally throughout her life, and he had a daughter, Anaga.

Miss Last was shy and softly-spoken, she treated children gently and considerately, and her pupils adored her. She had endless patience and coaxed even intractable infants to give of their best. Although she never had a formal training as a teacher, she was highly effective in teaching basic skills. By constant repetition the children became literate and numerate and, for particularly good behaviour, she would reward them by reading them stories. Favourites were those about Brer Rabbit and his friends, and Rudyard Kipling's 'Just So Stories'. Even for the older children, who had progressed up to the Big Room, at Christmas time or end of term Mrs Holdsworth would ask her to read to them, as a special treat.

Mrs Margaret Wright (school cook), Mrs Nell Righton (chairman of the school governors) and Miss Maud Last (infant teacher) circa 1980 in Maud's garden at the Leys, Didbrook (photograph provided by Miss Sarah Andrews).

After her father died, Maud continued to live at Stanway with her mother, whom she looked after until her death. She then moved to a smaller cottage in the Leys at Didbrook, where she enjoyed cooking, having a large garden and a Jack Russell terrier called Tug, and playing whist with Mrs Hilda Archer, Mrs Margaret Wright and Mrs Doris Daves. She took a great interest in the children of Francis and Dorothy Andrews, who lived in the next cottage, and often looked after Sarah so that Dorothy could go to work. Through Maud's efforts Sarah was able to read before she started school. Maud was also a great friend of my uncle, Frank Mann, who visited her regularly, especially as she became frail [5].

Unfortunately one day Maud and fell over a cable at home and fractured her hip. Following surgery she was never well enough to return home and she lived in an old people's home in Winchcombe until she died.

Miss Kathleen (Kay) Southerden
(head for 12 years, from 1958 to 1970)

After WW II Miss Southerden went to South Africa for some time and stayed outside Johannesburg. When she arrived at Didbrook, until a cottage became available for her in the Leys, she stayed with Mrs Margaret Wright, and they became close friends. She had a brother who visited occasionally.

Miss Southerden introduced the less formal approach to educating the junior children which became fashionable around that time. The HMI's report of October 10th 1960 included '*During the past two years the pattern of learning has undergone a change, the rigidity of passive class teaching has been superseded by a more personal and individual approach and the pupils are now participating more actively in their own education…..*' She continued the educational visits, mostly to local places such as Didbrook Fields Farm, Hailes Abbey, Winchcombe Potteries, Cheltenham Museum and Art Gallery, the Everyman Theatre and Cotswold Wildlife Park, but also to Bristol Zoo. She encouraged performances of drama and musical activities.

Unfortunately Miss Southerden had rheumatoid arthritis which significantly limited her mobility; she walked with a stick. However, she was able to participate in village activities, particularly the Women's Institute. She also took an interest in the welfare of the Ghurkas. After she retired she lived off the Bath Road in Cheltenham until her death [5].

Mrs Ada Holdsworth and Miss Kathleen Southerden (seated 3rd and 4th from the left) at a party of Stanway Women's Institute, during the 1970s. Others present include Mrs Gwen Moseley and Mrs Margaret Wright (seated 2nd and 5th from left) and, standing, left to right, Mrs Connie Shakespeare (school cleaner), Mrs Pike, Mrs Hilda Archer, Hon Violet Charteris (school governor), Mrs Kate Wright, Mrs Daisy Parrot, Mrs Wyniatt, Mrs Eileen Phillips, Mrs Violet Fathers and Mrs Cynthia Tredwell (photograph provided by Mr Glyn Wright).

Mr Ieuan GW Lewis
(head for almost 12 years, from 1970 to 1982).

Mr Lewis was born at Kidwelly, Carmarthenshire, on March 18th 1932. He was educated at Carmarthen Grammar School and then did two years National Service before undertaking his Teacher Training at Trinity College, Carmarthen for two years, completed in 1955. Ieuan taught from 1955 to 1957 in London and in 1958 he moved to Lacarno Road School in Tipton, Staffordshire, where he met his wife, Pat, who was also a teacher there. Ieuan and Pat were married in 1959 and had a daughter, Kate, born in 1965, the same year that Ieuan moved to Quarry Bank Junior Boys School; in January 1966, he transferred to a similar school in Wordsley (both were Staffordshire schools).

On September 9th, 1970 Ieuan became Headmaster of Didbrook School. For the first 3 months he and his family lived in one of the cottages in the Leys at Didbrook and they then moved to a house in Winchcombe.

Mrs Lewis remembers that when they arrived Didbrook School did not have a telephone. Fortunately Ieuan had a car, so he could drive any child who was injured or unwell home or to hospital, as necessary. The school was still heated by a huge black stove surrounded by a substantial fireguard. The heat produced was inadequate and the stove was eventually replaced by storage heaters; also the ceiling of the school room was lowered to reduce heat loss. She remembers numerous problems with the terrapin classroom, which eventually collapsed, fortunately when no one was inside.

Pupils and staff at Didbrook School in summer 1981:
Front (1st) row: Adam Hensley, Ellen Brooks, Stella Green, Sarah Gregory, Sarah Collins, Scott Walford, Cherry?, Kevin Harris, Matthew Harvey
2nd row: Samantha Turpitt, Mrs Jane Brooks (secretary), Mrs Rosemary Davis (cook), Mrs Pam Linari-Linholm, Mr Ieuan Lewis (head master), Mrs Barbara Trickey, Mrs Connie Shakespeare, Donna Roberts, Ben Greenhalf
3rd row: Wendy Green, Tara Gamble, Brett Brooks, Bryony Cook, Tania Collins, Rachel Pugh, Joanna Heritage, Becky Foley
4th row: Rachel Beard, Lucy Burrows, Hannah Ryland, Geraint Thomas, Ian Harris, Edward Walker, Nicky Smith, Helen Pugh, Stephen Andrews.

The Five a side teams after the Match against Brook County Primary School in 1973. Didbrook School's players are in blue, left to right: Robert Harris, Nigel Smith, Chris Fisher, Tony Clark, Gary Curtis

Ieuan was particularly keen to encourage sports and he set up matches eg 'five a side football', with neighbouring schools and also with Brook County Primary School, Wordsley, Staffordshire. He introduced swimming, initially in a plastic contraption at Winchcombe and later at Evesham Swimming Pool. He encouraged the children to play recorders and to sing and enjoyed reading to them.

Following problems with his heart, unfortunately Ieuan had to take early retirement in July 1982 and he died on January 7th 1995 [6].

Mr David Sanders B.Ed (Hons) (head for 19 years, from 1982 to 2001)

Mr Sanders was born on November 15th, 1950 in Beverley, East Yorkshire and was educated at Beverley Grammar School and St Paul's College, Cheltenham, graduating in 1974. He taught at Bishop's Cleeve Primary School from 1974 to 1982 and then moved to the headship of Didbrook School.

David was particularly keen on sport and introduced a wide range of activities, including rounders, cricket, football, netball, hockey, swimming and cross-country running, often in competition with pupils from other local schools. He also took many children on educational school trips, some of them residential. Among his memories of these was an occasion in York when the fire alarm of their hotel went off in the middle of the night. The children were so exhausted by their activities during the day that none of them woke up, so David had to rouse them from their beds and take them to safety. Fortunately it was a false alarm! The week had involved taking 12 children (including his son Gary, aged 5 and daughter Ellen, aged 3) together with his wife Jill who was a qualified teacher, by minibus to York, where they stayed at St Paul's Hotel. Their activities included visiting the Yorkshire and Railway Museums, Yorvic, walking around the walls and swimming - 'One of the best weeks of my life'.

There were many changes and challenges during David's time at Didbrook School, which included several attempts by the LEA to close it; all were successfully resisted (see Chapter 1). In order to improve the school by modernising and enlarging it, he had to make considerable economies; these helped to pay for the two new classrooms and other work which were completed in 2003. These were achieved at considerable personal cost. For example he himself would often do minor repairs, such as plumbing, out of school hours to avoid paying a plumber and did not take any pay rises for some years.

David also worked hard with the parents' association, the Friends of Didbrook School, to raise money for the school's funds. For example, on June 7th 1992 Mr and Mrs Geoffrey Peel kindly allowed their beautiful garden at the vicarage to be used for a summer fete at which over £700 were raised. Some of this came from offering the children, at a price, a chance to soak their headmaster, who was restrained in stocks!

David had to implement the frequent new Education Acts and other government directives, which included the National Curriculum, Local Management of Schools (LMS), open enrolment of pupils (who had previously come from a defined catchment area including Buckland, Laverton, Stanton, Stanway, Didbrook and Hailes), and the introduction of Standard Attainment Tests (SATs) and of local projects with other small schools (Toddington, Oakhill and Gretton). In addition he was successful in working closely with Winchcombe School and used it as a base for theatre groups and other initiatives. He also introduced school uniforms. When asked what he particularly enjoyed about working at Didbrook School, David said that it was being able to build up such a good relationship with the children, based upon mutual respect. He also had fond memories of his work with the governors, recollecting with affection the long-standing Clerk to the Governors, Frank Hughes, who always brought a bottle of sherry to the meetings to share with everyone.

After his retirement David and his wife Jill moved to Bishop's Cleeve [7, 8].

Pupils and staff at Didbrook School in 1985:

Front (1st) row:
Benjamin Turpitt, Stuart Beard, Matthew Greenhalf, Emma Poole, Richard Ryland, Joanna Higgins, Kelly Law, Michael Green, Daniel Roberts, Jonathan Metherall, Sam Gregory

2nd row:
Adam Hensley, Alice Potterton, Mrs Jenny Brooks (cleaner), Mrs Janet Freeman, Mr David Sanders (head master), Mrs Jane Brooks, Mrs Rosemary Davis, Ellen Brooks, Samantha Turpitt

3rd row:
Nicholas Pankhurst, Sarah Gregory, Helen Pugh, Steven Andrews, Hannah Ryland, Stella Green, Nicholas Smith, Lucy Burrows, Christopher ?, Scott Walford, Donna Andrews

4th row:
Paul Burrows, Richard Poole, Kirsty Johns, Matthew Harvey, Alex Metherall, Sarah Collins, Donna Roberts, Angela Pitt, Rachel Beard, Kevin Harris, Ben Greenhalf, Pippa Harvey.

*Soak the headmaster
(David Sanders)!
Fete at Didbrook
Vicarage, June 7th,
1992.*

Mrs Georgette Williams serving food and drinks.

Mrs Gillian Gregory pouring tea

Pupils and staff at Didbrook School in 1994/5, in their new uniforms:
1st row: Zachariah ?, Maria Harris, Drew Leitch, Zac Butler, Alexandra
Yeadon, Joey Gwynn-Jones, Clara Hill
2nd row: unknown, Tim Brown, Stephanie Keogh-Golish, Emily Hill, Daniel
Harding, Luke Butler, Lucy Boulton, Carrie Clark, Francis Wilkinson,
Leanne Rose
3rd row: Kevin Mower, Darren Boulton, Georgina Hall, Toby Shaw, Mrs Sally
Higgins, Mrs Jill Sanders, Mr David Sanders (head master), Mrs Jane Brooks,
Gary Harris, Claire Elliott, Matthew Cooper, Robert Gwynn-Jones
4th row: Mrs Janet Freeman, Nick Millard, Amy Wilkinson, Rachel
Boulton,
David Williams, Kate Widdows, Richard Hall, Martyn Beard, Ashley
Mitchell, Martin Hill, Amy Boulton, Mrs Georgette Williams (cook)

Mr David Ogden, BA (Hons) (head for 6 years from 2001 to 2007)

David was born on April 16th, 1960 in Leeds and was educated at Weedon Primary School, Campion Comprehensive School, Bugbrooke (a village in Northamptonshire similar to Winchcombe) and he then studied sociology at North Staffordshire Polytechnic (now Staffordshire University) graduating in 1982. From 1984 to 1985 he studied at Bath College of Higher Education to obtain his PGCE (Postgraduate Certificate of Education).

Pupils and staff at Didbrook School in 2003:
1st row: Lloyd Culpepper, Molly Alexander, Callum James, Tom Stanford, Billie Turner, Jerrin Nixon, Sam Culpepper
2nd row: Mali Symons, Mrs Jane Brooks, Mrs Jane Merchant, Mr David Ogden (head master), Mrs Sue Brewin, Mrs Nikki Webb, Joe White
3rd row: Scott Parker, Donai Turner, Lily Hamer, Alex Porter, Sam Hayling, Fern Baldwin, Martha Gregory, Liam Mustoe
4th row: Bradley White, Lucinda White, Tom Wallis, Lewis Corder, Rosie Widdows, Jodi Brooks, Holly James, Holly Brooks
5th row: Khalen Nixon, Jack Doran, Tom Garwood, Kirsty Tolley, Daniel Mustoe, Duncan Whiston, Phoebe Harding.

David taught at primary schools in Enfield, Middlesex from 1985 to 1988. He then moved to the primary section of Greengates School, an international school for children aged 4 to 18 years in Mexico City, where he met his wife, Denise, who was also teaching there. After they returned to the UK in 1993, David taught in Essex, at Tilbury until 1997 and at Wickford until 2001.

When he became head of Didbrook Primary School, David and his family lived at Stanway and their daughter Clodagh attended the School. After Clodagh moved to Cotswold School at Bourton-on-the-Water, they moved to a house there and David commuted to Didbrook daily.

As soon as he became head, David had to oversee the extensive remodelling of the school which was carried out during 2001-3. This necessitated transferring the classes to the former Winchcombe Junior School for the autumn and spring terms, 2001-2. He also encouraged the mother of one of his pupils to develop a school garden in which the pupils could work and learn.

David retired from Didbrook School at the end of the autumn term of 2007 in order to take up an appointment as head of Temple Guiting School in January 2008 [9].

Mrs Lesley Marriott became Acting Head of Didbrook School until its closure in August 2008 and in September 2008 she became the Head of the new Isbourne Valley School, formed by the amalgamation of Didbrook and Toddington Schools; the Reception class and Infants were then taught at Toddington and the Juniors at Didbrook.

SOURCES

1.   Discussions with Mrs Elizabeth Brett
2.   Discussions with Mr Bryan Markwell
3.   Didbrook Parish Records, Register of burials 1813-2007
4.   Interview with Mr Horace Holmes
5.   Interview with Mr and Mrs Francis Andrews
6.   Interview with Mrs Pat Lewis
7.   Interview with Mrs David Sanders
8.   Interview with Mrs Alison Whiston
9.   Interview with Mr David Ogden

Table 4.
Teachers at Didbrook School

Head Teachers	Dates
Mrs Ann Harrison	Uncertain, included 1851 and 1861
Miss Kate Miller	Uncertain, included 1870
Miss Mary Frost	Uncertain, included 1874
Mrs Mary Alcock	October 6th 1879 to December 31st 1915
Miss Mary Alcock (temporary head)	January 10th 1916 to February 29th 1916
Miss (or Mrs) Kathleen Beesley	March 6th 1916 to April 30th 1919
Miss Mary Alcock (temporary supply teacher)	May 1st 1919 to May 30th 1919
Mrs (or Miss) Lizzie Evans	June 2nd 1919 to April 27th 1921
Miss Mary Alcock (temporary supply teacher)	May 2nd to 31st 1921
Miss Beatrice Prothero	June 1st 1921 to July 28th 1921
Mr John Wood Maybury	August 30th 1921 to March 20th 1922
Mr (?) FC Smith (supply teacher)	March 27th 1922 to August 4th 1922
Mr Cedric E Stagg	September 4th 1922 to August 10th 1923
Mr Lindsey Norman Gay	September 10th 1923 to May 17th 1929
Mrs Ada A Holdsworth	May 27th 1929 to December 20th 1957
Ms AL Jackson (County supply teacher)	January 7th 1958 to April 2nd 1958
Miss Kathleen Southerden	April 21st 1958 to July 24th 1970
Mr Ieuan GW Lewis	September 9th 1970 to July 23rd 1982
Mr David Sanders	September 2nd 1982 to August 31st 2001
Mr David Ogden	September1st 2001 to December 31st 2007
Mrs Lesley Marriott (Acting head)	January 1st 2008 to August 31st 2008

Other Teachers (and Nursery nurses/assistants)

Miss Florence Stanford	(Assistant Teacher) November 2nd 1903 to December 4th 1905
Miss Mary Alcock	(Assistant Teacher, from St Alban's School, Birmingham) December 5th 1905 to September 28th 1906
Miss Charlotte (Lottie)Alcock	(Supplementary Teacher) October 1st 1906 to March 31st 1911
Miss Jennie (Jane?) Alcock	(Supplementary Teacher, later Assistant Teacher) April 3rd 1911 to ?
Miss Bessie Alcock	(Temporary Supplementary Teacher) Nov 27th to Dec 1st 1911
Miss Frost	(Infant teacher in 1919?)
Miss Maud Last	(Supplementary Teacher, Infant class) August 31st 1921 to December 18th 1953 and June 6th 1955 to July 26th 1963
Miss Edith Fielding	(Supplementary Teacher) November 1st 1921 to January 30th 1931
Miss Margaret Innes	(Pupil-Teacher) February 2nd 1925 to May 31st 1926
Mr Geoffrey HL Moulton	(Student Teacher) September 3rd 1928 to August 1st 1929
Miss Jessica Edmonds	(Probationer Teacher) June 18th 1934 to September 30th 1935
Mr Wyndham H Davies	(Teacher) April 8th 1940 to August 12th 1941
Mrs Daisy Beatrice Philpott	(Teacher) September 15th 1941 to April 5th 1944
Mrs J Leenders(née Blandford)	(Supplementary Assistant) February 8th 1945 to April 30th 1945
Mrs Barbara Trickey	(Permanent Supply Teacher, Infants) September 9th 1963 to July 22nd 1966, and then worked as a Part-time teacher from September 7th 1966 to July 23rd, 1982
Mrs Paula Mary Humphries	(Part-time Teacher) January 6th 1965 to ?
Mrs Butterworth	(Temporary teacher) September 5th 1966 to October 21st 1966
Mrs Minett	(Infants' Teacher) October 31st 1966 to December 22nd, 1966

Mrs Porter	(Temporary Assistant Teacher) from January 4th, 1967 to March 22nd, 1967 and from June 5th, 1967 to July 26th, 1968
Mrs Joan A Peeters	(Temporary qualified assistant- infants) from April 10th to 11th, 1967
Mrs Finch	(Assistant Teacher, Infants) from April 24th to May 26th, 1967
Mrs Ison	(Infants Teacher) from March 1968 (possibly did not take up the post) to ?
Mrs Harman	(Infants Teacher) from September 4th, 1968 to December 21st, 1973
Mrs Pam Linari-Linholm	(Infants) from January 9th 1974 to April 2nd, 1982.
Mrs Ross	(Remedial Teacher, one day per week) from September 7th, 1978 to
Mrs Janet Freeman	(Infants) April 19th 1982 to August 2002
Miss Helena Millin	(Part-time Teacher) from September 9th 1982 to December 16th 1982
Mrs Carol Rhodes	(Part-time Teacher) from January 12th 1983 to October 24th 1986
Mrs Appleby	(Part-time Teacher) from September 3rd 1986 to December 21st, 1989.
Miss Paula Wainwright	(Nursery Nurse) September 8th 1986 to July 20th 1988
Mrs Boniface	(Part-time PE Teacher) from December 1st 1986 to ?
Mrs Jill Sanders	(Part-time Teacher) from December 2nd, 1986 to August 31st, 1998
Mrs Brown	(Part-time Support Teacher) from January 7th 1987 to ?
Miss Mills	(Nursery Nurse) from September 12th 1988 to July 20th 1990
Mrs Heather Taylor	(Part-time teacher) from January 8th 1990 to June 1993
Mrs Sally A Higgins	(Nursery Assistant) from September 4th 1990 to1995, then became Part-time Specialist Teacher Assistant until December 18th 1998
Mrs J Elaine Webb	(Part-time SEN teacher) from September 31st 1991 to August 31st, 1998
Mrs Jane Merchant	(Part-time teacher) from September 1st 1998 to August 31st 2006

Mrs Susan Brewin	(Part-time Teacher's Assistant/Learning Support Worker and qualified NNEB) from January 1999 to 2003, then Part-time Infants Teacher (2003 to present)
Mrs. Tracey Poole	(Part-time Teacher's Assistant) September - December 2001
Mrs Amanda Reynolds	(Learning Support Worker) from 2002 to December 31st, 2004
Mrs Nikki Webb	(Learning Support Worker) from 2003 to August 31st 2008
Mrs Clarice Berlouis	(Learning Support Worker) from February 2005 to 2007
Miss Mandy Young	(Student Teacher, of juniors) Jan/Feb 2005 to Easter 2005
Mr Graham Murray	(Juniors Teacher) from September 2006 to August 31st 2008
Mrs May Podd	(Learning Support Worker) from 2007 to August 31st 2008

Also, Mrs Jill Sanders often filled in for sick leave and other staff absences committees throughout her husband's time as Head Teacher, ie from September 2nd, 1982 to August 31st 2001.

Monitors

Miss Mabel Martin	April 4th 1898 to September 26th 1900
Miss Mary Alcock	September 26th 1900 to September 27th, 1901
Miss Olive Martin	October 21st 1901 to ?
Miss Flossie Martin	1902 (dates?)
Miss Lottie Alcock	1903 (dates?)
Miss Bessie Drury Alcock	November 30th 1903 to ?
Miss Annie Horlick	March 6th 1916 to April 27th 1917
Miss Maud Last	May 1st 1917 to July 28th 1921
Miss Barbara Mason	October 7th 1935 to March 24th 1937
Miss Joan Blandford	April 5th 1937 to June 9th 1941
Miss Eira Dowding	June 1st 1941 to August 31st 1941

Chapter 4.
PATRONAGE AND GOVERNANCE AT DIDBROOK SCHOOL

And he who gives a child a treat
Makes joy-bells ring in Heaven's street,
And he who gives a child a home
Builds palaces in Kingdom come.

John Masefield (1878-1967), The Everlasting Mercy.

PATRONAGE

The Tracy family

Didbrook School was built and owned by Charles Hanbury-Tracy, 3rd Baron Sudeley of Toddington Manor. He died in 1877 and his role was taken on by the 4th Baron, Charles Douglas [1]. Their stewards visited the school regularly to inspect the registers and deal with any problems, such as repairs and redecoration to the building and care of the grounds. Lady Sudeley took a great interest in the school and around Christmas would usually invite all the children to a tea and entertainments at Toddington Manor. At another tea party in August 1884 she presented prizes to the children who had had the best attendance. Also, on June 21st 1887 she invited all the children to Toddington Manor for a tea party to mark Queen Victoria's Golden Jubilee.

The Charteris family

After the exchange of land in 1890 between the Toddington and Stanway estates, the ownership of the school passed to Francis Charteris, 10th Earl of Wemyss and March. Lord Wemyss' son Hugo, Lord Elcho, sent his agent Mr CH Smith to make his first visit to the school on December 9th 1889, to find a way to improve the heating. On Christmas Eve 1890 Lady Elcho gave a Christmas tree function for the children at Stanway 'Mansion' and this became an annual event. She also gave tea parties for the schoolchildren each summer. From time to time Lady Elcho would visit the school, often bringing along friends or house guests; for example on January 15th 1909 Lady Violet Manners, Miss Dorothy Vernon, Lord Vernon, Hon Percy Wyndham and Hon Guy Charteris, who heard the children sing.

In February 1910 Lady Elcho sent Miss Warren, a young lady from a London College, to the school to teach the children Morris dancing and on June 4th the children with their mothers were invited to tea at Stanway House to give a display of Morris dancing and organised Infants games.

Over the years the children from Didbrook School participated in many charitable and other events at Stanway House. For example, in 1911 the girls made garments, cushions, kettle-holders and other needlework for the Church Sale of Work at Stanway, towards the cost of repairing and hanging Didbrook Church Bells and for an Organ fund, and the children gave an Entertainment in Stanway House. Also, on March 8th 1912 the children were invited to attend the christening of the baby son of Lady Violet (Letty) Charteris at Stanway Church (this child, Francis David, subsequently became the 12th Earl of Wemyss).

In 1914 the 10th Earl of Wemyss and March died. He was succeeded by his son Hugo, Lord Elcho, who then became the 11th Earl, and he and the Countess continued to support the school, as they had done as Lord and Lady Elcho. However, no Christmas and summer parties for the children appear to have taken place during the war years or for some time afterwards. Tragically two of Lord and Lady Wemyss' sons were killed during the Great War. Yvo died at Loos in 1915 and Ego, Lord Elcho in Sinai in 1916.

In December 1924 Lady Wemyss visited the school to see an exhibition of the children's work which was attended by about 60 people, mostly parents, but also by Miss Wilkinson (correspondent), Rev Bennett (a Manager), Miss Wedgwood and the Rev and Mrs H B Allen. In January 1925 a party was held for the children at Stanway House. Also, garden parties/fetes were held there in 1926 and 1927.

On July 24th 1929 the school was closed so that the children could take part in the Stanway Pageant in aid of Winchcombe Hospital, and the following day school closed early so that they could go to the Stanway Carnival. On December 18th that year an Open Afternoon was attended *'by Lady Wemyss and many parents. After inspection of the children's daily notebooks, handwork and needlework, a programme of folk songs and carols, country dancing and verses was received appreciatively'.*

On May 30th 1932 a concert was held by the children to raise money for a visit to the Three Counties Show at Gloucester. There was a large and appreciative audience, which included the Countess of Wemyss, Rev HB

Meeting of the local branch of the Royal Antediluvian Order of Buffaloes at Stanway House. Rev Herbert Bancroft Allen, curate and then vicar of Didbrook, Hailes and Stanway from 1912 to 1945, and a manager of Didbrook School, is in the middle of the front row, wearing a tabard (photograph provided by Mrs Morna Fisher).

Stanway Pageant, July 24th 1929 (photograph provided by Mrs Doreen Nurden)

and Mrs Allen and Mrs Alcock, and £3-0-5½ was raised. In addition, Lady Wemyss gave £3 to pay for railway fares and reserved seats for 14 children to go to a matinée at Stratford Memorial Theatre.

Both the Earl and the Countess of Wemyss died in 1937 and Stanway House was requisitioned during WWII to house Miss Kerr-Sanders' Secretarial College which was evacuated there from London. After the war the college returned to London and Lady Violet Benson (formerly Lady Elcho, the widow of Ego Charteris) and her second husband Guy Benson came to live at Stanway House. They stayed there and continued the tradition of hospitality to the school children until their deaths (in 1971 and 1974 respectively), since when this role has been undertaken by Lord Neidpath (now Lord Wemyss) and his family.

National and other Events

On many occasions national events were celebrated at Stanway House, with participation by the school children. Thus, for the Silver Jubilee of George V and Queen Mary on Monday 6th May 1935 there were sports and tea there and the children gave a programme of country dances and songs. The children also participated in the VE Day celebration in 1945, at which there were children's games, a bonfire upon which an effigy of Hitler was burnt, and a dance in the Tithe Barn.

On June 2nd 1953 the school children participated in the Celebrations to mark the Coronation of Queen Elizabeth II. These were held in the grounds of Stanway House and in the Tithe Barn. After a service in Stanway Church there were sports for the children and adults, tea in the Tithe Barn, a Punch and Judy show, fancy dress parades for children and adults, folk dancing and songs, a tug of war and dancing in the Tithe Barn. Each child was presented with a coronation mug made at Winchcombe Pottery.

On June 7th 1977 Stanway House was the venue for the celebrations of Queen Elizabeth II's Silver Jubilee. The children sang a song for each country in the British Isles, performed two dances and a novelty item depicting St George and the Dragon, and finished with a Gymnastics display. The Queen's Golden Jubilee in 2002 was also celebrated at Stanway House, and in 2005 Lord Neidpath marked the 200th anniversary of the Battle of Trafalgar by giving an entertaining lecture to the children about Nelson and the battle.

Tea in the Tithe Barn during the Coronation Celebrations, June 2nd, 1953
(photograph provided by Mr Glyn Wright)

The fancy dress parade for adults:
Back row: unknown, Austen Righton, unknown, unknown,
Hannah Holmes, Eric Righton, Mrs Tillie Hardiman, unknown
Front row: Elizabeth Holmes, Jean Nightingale, unknown, Ann Holmes,
Mrs Margaret Wright, MrsViolet Fathers, Marjorie Righton
(photograph was provided by Glyn Wright)

In Stanway Tithe Barn, awaiting the presentation of Winchcombe Pottery mugs to the children at the Coronation Celebrations, June 2nd, 1953: Mr WF (Bill) Mann (chairman of Parish Council and School Manager), Guy Charteris (School Manager and Correspondent) and Mr Derrick Anderson (Honorary Treasurer). (The photograph was provided by Philip Mann).

Rounders being played Stanway Cricket Field, 1993. The pavilion, erected by Sir James Barrie, is seen in the background.

Mr David Sanders and Lord Neidpath presenting the prizes at the end of term party, July 1991, when the success of the campaign to save the school from closure was celebrated.

The party's barbeque, July 1991; Mrs Alison Whiston, Chairman of the Governors, is on the far left.

The balloon going up, assisted by David Sanders and Sally Higgins, July 1991

Jack O'Green (Andrew York) and the Queens of the May (Lucinda White and Fern Baldwin) at the May Day celebration held jointly by pupils of Didbrook and Toddington Schools at Stanway House in 2006 (JRM)

The procession leaving the courtyard (JRM)

The procession passing the lake (JRM)

Lord Neidpath crowning Jack O'Green watched by Lady Neidpath and the May Queens (JRM)

Dancing around the maypole (JRM)

The Wemyss family allowed Stanway House and its grounds, including the Cricket Ground, to be used on many occasions by the school, for sports and other events, including for tournaments to which other schools were invited.

In 1991 Lord Neidpath played a major part in the campaign to save the school from closure and this success was celebrated at the end of term party in July, where he and Mr Sanders presented the prizes.

On May 1st 2006, during the negotiations which led to the amalgamation of Didbrook and Toddington Schools, the children of the two schools held a May Day Festival in the gardens of Stanway House at which they had a procession led by a May Queen from each school and the children jointly performed a display of Maypole dancing. Lord and Lady Neidpath crowned the two May Queens and Jack o' Green and there were a children's fancy dress dog show and a number of side shows.

Financial and other support

The Wemyss family, and before them the Tracy family, provided significant financial support to the school over many years, usually bearing the cost of repairs and charging only a modest rent for the building (since 2000 just a 'peppercorn rent'). In 1987 a sports field for the school was also provided free of rent by Lord Neidpath.

Since they acquired ownership of the school in 1890 there has always been a member of the Wemyss family on the Managing/Governing body.

GOVERNANCE

From 1879, when Mrs Alcock started her Log books, or earlier, the school was under the management of the Vicar, then Rev WD Stanton, who lived at Toddington, and his curate, Rev J Fountain, who lived at Didbrook vicarage, and Lord Sudeley of Toddington Manor. The clergy visited the school very frequently, at least once a week, and Lord Sudeley's steward, Mr Owen, visited at intervals. The clergy checked the registers and undertook religious instruction including the catechism, and some also taught other subjects. If the head teacher was ill, the vicar or curate would open the school and take the register. They also brought in stationery, books, slates, pencils, pens, ink and other necessities and the vicar's wife supplied materials for the girls' sewing classes and brought the teachers' pay cheques.

There was an annual Diocesan inspection, when Rev Charles H Awdry examined the children in Religious knowledge; his successors included Revs WH Cotes, AW Douglas, FW Cropper, Ponsonby Sullivan, HB Allen and GN Bennett.

From 1879, or earlier, the children sat annual government examinations in the 'Three R's' and every year there was an inspection by one of Her Majesty's Inspectors. Before Mrs Alcock's appointment in 1879 the school may not have been eligible for government grants, because she was probably its first fully qualified (Certificated) teacher. The school was examined for a grant for the first time on February 8th 1881, by Mr J Percival Bateman. Following the Newcastle Commission's report (1862) grants depended upon the number of attendances, the HMI's report and examination results [2]. So Mrs Alcock was assiduous in recording reasons for absences and the results of school examinations and Mr George Haslum, the Attendance (Relieving) officer for the School Board at Winchcombe, visited the school frequently, took the names of absentees and the farmers who were employing them, and contacted the parents of frequent offenders. On a number of occasions he reported parents of absentees to the School Board and they were fined. Mr Haslum retired in 1901 and his successors were Messrs Woodward, Moulton, Dubber and Webb.

When in 1890 the school became part of the Stanway Estate, Lord Wemyss and his heir Lord Elcho, their agents and the clergy continued to govern the school in a similar way. Implementing Balfour's Education Act of 1902 [2] necessitated increasing the number of managers to six, to include other local people. One of the managers, or someone appointed to do so, acted as 'Correspondent' and kept minutes, dealt with correspondence with the Education Authority at Gloucester and helped with administration.

From 1981, instead of Managers, a similar committee of Governors managed the school and were supported by a clerk. The Governors included representatives of the Local Education Authority, the Community, parents of the pupils, the head teacher and staff. The Appendix shows the names of those who served the school as Clergy, Managers, Correspondents, Governors and Clerks between 1879 and 2008 and also the HMIs.

APPENDIX

CLERGY of parishes who helped to run the school from 1850s to 2008:
Didbrook, Hailes and Toddington Rectors: William Whalley, WD Stanton.
Didbrook and Hailes Vicars: Herbert Bancroft Allen (1912 - 1945)
Curates: Hudson B Pruen, H Hall, R Gledowe Hurle, James Fountain, E Mogridge, FF Collin, AS Lister, J A Clarke, RCB Gray, JA Williams, Hubert Bancroft Allen, CJ Farr, Richard F Mallam
Didbrook, Hailes and Stanway Vicars: Richard F Mallam, Herbert Bancroft Allen, GN Bennett, AD Guyer Bidlake
Curate: Jack Lawton
Didbrook, Hailes, Stanway, Toddington, Wormington and Dumbleton Rector/Priest in charge: Peter CL Richards
Didbrook, Hailes and Stanway Vicars: Canon Robert W Miles, Michael G Bennett, Keith L Bruton
Didbrook, Hailes, Stanway and Toddington Vicar: Nicola Arthy

MANAGERS 1879 to 1980 (teachers not listed)

Rev WD Stanton (from 1879 or earlier, until his death in 1912), Mr Owen (Lord Sudeley's steward), Lord Elcho, Lord Elcho/Wemyss's agents (Messrs CH Smith, Harvey, A Weston, Mitchell and John Last), Rev HB Allen, Messrs Scarlett, Blake, Horace Horlick, W Mann, Rev GN Bennett, Mr HJ Archer, Mrs Mary Alcock, Lt Col Knight, Rev ADG Bidlake, Hon Guy Charteris, Mrs E (Nell) Righton, Messrs WF Mann, J Horlick, Mrs (Lady) Peacock, Mrs S Anderson, Messrsr F Hughes, J Richards, Foley, C Dickins, Mrs S Sadler, Mrs Harper.

Chairmen

(not known for earlier years) Lt Col Knight, Mrs (Lady) Peacock, Mrs E (Nell) Righton, Messrs W F Mann, J Horlick, C Dickins.

Official correspondents

Rev Stanton, Rev CJ Farr, Rev RF Mallam, Mr JC Mitchell, Rev HB Allen (1912 to 1922), Mr J Last, Miss WJ Wilkinson, Rev GN Bennett, Messrs W Mann, S Wood, Hon Guy Charteris, Mrs(Lady) K Peacock and Mr Frank Hughes (from 1967 for 25 years, including period as Clerk to Governors).

GOVERNORS 1981 to 2008 (teaching staff not listed)

Messrs C Dickins, WF Mann, F Hughes (clerk), Mrs Harper, Mrs Susan Anderson, Mrs S Sadler, Mr Foley, Mrs Walford, PC D Collins, Catherine Lady Neidpath, Rev J Lawton, Mrs Walford, Mr C Higgins, Mrs Strickland, Mrs J Uedelhoven, Mrs Sheila Anderson, Lord Neidpath (later became Lord Wemyss), Mrs G Strickland, Mrs J Alford, Mrs S Brown, Mrs N Gwyn-Jones, Mr M Harding, Mrs E Fenton, Mrs A Whiston, Mrs J Ward, Mrs Bourne, Messrs J White, J Harding, D Hayling, Prof JR Mann, Mrs G Edwards, Mr R Allen, Ms R Court.

Chairmen

Mr C Dickins, Mrs Gwyn-Jones, Mr C Higgins, Mrs A Whiston, Mr D Hayling.

Clerks

Mr F Hughes, Mrs JE Harris, Ms H Wilkinson, Mr G Sanders, Mrs T Symons, Ms J Gommer.

HER/HIS MAJESTY'S INSPECTORS from 1881 onwards:

Messrs J Percival Bateman, JP Baliner, J Waite, F B de Sausmarez, JSD Campbell, WH Bulley, C More, F Harvey, J Leicester, LS Wood, Parker, PW Scott, EE Bessey, Miss Ffinch, Mr R Tanner, Miss Perry, Mr Tompkins, Mr Philips, Miss Harris, Dr Plotts, Miss Clarke, Miss Barrett, Messrs Auty, Kingston, Harrap, Miss Ramirez, Messrs Ungoed-Thomas, Agnew, Collier and C Rogers and J Gill.

From 1993 the OFSTED system took over and the first inspectors were Mr C Rogers and Ms J Spouse.

SOURCES

1. H J McCarthy and M Prance (edited by L Cheshire). A history and memories of Toddington - A Gloucestershire Village. BookPublishing World, 2006

2. Curtis SJ. History of Education in Great Britain, 7th Edition, University Tutorial Press, London, 1967.

Chapter 5.
CURRICULUM AND ACHIEVEMENTS

Reading maketh a full man, conference a ready man,
and writing an exact man.
Francis Bacon (1561-1626). Religious Meditations. Of Studies.

Studies serve for delight, for ornament, and for ability.
Francis Bacon. Religious Meditations. Of Studies.

For knowledge itself is power.
Francis Bacon. Religious Meditations. Of Heresies.

National trends in the 19th century

The first attempts to regulate the curriculum taught in schools followed the Reform Bill of 1832. This provided the first government grants, which were initially towards the cost of building school houses for educating the children of the poorer classes. Subsequently grants could be requested towards the running costs of schools provided by voluntary bodies and, from 1839, these were overseen by Her Majesty's Inspectors. The (Duke of) Newcastle Commission's report of 1862 included a Revised Code, whereby grants depended on the average number of attendances at each school and the HMI's annual report. The Revised Code introduced six Standards of attainment in the 'Three R's' - Reading Writing and Arithmetic. The syllabus for each Standard is shown in the table. Every year the HMI recommended the topics known as 'Object lessons' to be studied each term, following the national guidelines. For example in 1886 the objects were: salt, a letter, gardens, candles, thimbles, needles, teapot, oak tree, snowdrop, owl, hedgehog, forest, wind and stars [1].

All the children in a school were grouped according to their attainment and studied for the appropriate Standard. Examinations were held annually. If a child failed to pass an examination, 2s 8d was forfeited from the school's grant for each subject failed. Other recommendations for receipt of a full grant included satisfactory condition of the school, the head teacher to be certificated, various conditions regarding the number of pupil teachers and assistant teachers be complied with, all the girls to receive instruction in plain needlework and a log book be kept up to date[1].

Table 5.

REVISED CODE STANDARDS, 1862

Subject	Standard I	Standard II	Standard III	Standard IV	Standard V	Standard VI
Reading	Narrative monosyllables.	One of the narratives next in order after monosyllables in an elementary reading book used in the school.	A short paragraph from an elementary reading book used in the school.	A short paragraph from a more advanced reading book used in the school.	A few lines of poetry from a reading book used in the first class of the school.	A short ordinary paragraph in a newspaper, or other modern narrative.
Writing	Form on blackboard or slate, from dictation, letters, capital and small, manuscript.	Copy in manuscript character a line of print.	A sentence from the same paragraph slowly read once and then dictated in single words.	A sentence slowly dictated once by a few words at a time, from the same book, but not from the paragraph read.	A sentence slowly dictated once, by a few words at a time, from a reading book used in the first class of the school.	Another short ordinary paragraph in a newspaper, or other modern narrative, slowly dictated once by a few words at a time.
Arithmetic	Form on blackboard or slate, from dictation, figures up to 20; name at sight figures up to 20; add and subtract figures up to 10, orally, from examples on blackboard.	A sum in simple addition or subtraction, and the multiplication table.	A sum in any simple rule as far as short division (Inclusive).	A sum in compound rules (money).	A sum in compound rules (common weights and measures).	A sum in practice or bills of parcels.

- 90 -

Implementation in Didbrook and Stanway Schools

The Log Books reveal that most of the provisions of the Newcastle Commission's Report were implemented, although in the early years it was not always possible to obtain and retain certificated teachers and sufficient other staff.

Thus, when Mrs Alcock became head of Didbrook School she wrote:
'On October 6th 1879 I opened Didbrook Mixed School (signed) Mary Alcock Certificated Teacher.
October 6 - 10. The children have just had five weeks Harvest holidays. Twenty four children present. No Log book in the school. No proper entries in the Admission register. Scarcely any of the Infants know any letters or figures - children above seven are very backward.
October 13 - 17. The Rev WD Stanton visited. I have classed the children into four Divisions. Viz: Infants (Classes I and II) Standards I, II, and III (Clearly none of the children had reached the higher Standards then); *also drawn out a Time Table allowing time for Grammar and Geography to be taught.'* Mrs Alcock also taught religious education, sewing, darning, knitting and songs.

The first inspection by an HMI took place on February 8th 1881. There were 26 boys and 20 girls present, aged from 4 to 13 years. They sang a number of songs *'very nicely'* and the 23 children aged 7 years and above were examined in reading, writing and arithmetic. Twenty-two passed in all subjects and one girl failed just arithmetic. The inspector's report, however, cautioned *'that the school is now being examined for a grant for the first time, and that some of the children are in standards very low for their age.'* However, a year later, the HMI's report stated *'its hardworking mistress is doing the same successful work as heretofore. Its quality is satisfactory throughout'* and in 1883 he stated *'The school is in good order, and the results of examinations are a strong proof of the teacher's conscientious diligence...'*

In 1889 14 of the 17 pupils who were examined passed in all three subjects, among them being four of Mrs Alcock's own children, Grace, Edith, Ada and Charles. Mrs Alcock's hard work over the decade since her appointment in raising the standard of the children's work resulted in the school being awarded government grants.

In 1890 the Code for grants to schools was revised by abolishing the grant for the three R's, raising the fixed grant and retaining other grants only for specific subjects [1]. Mrs Alcock recorded in September 1891 that the children now had *'the advantage of free education for the first time'*. The HMI's report for 1897 stated *'This school continues to maintain its character for good and intelligent work. It would be a good thing to appoint someone to help Mrs Alcock'*. Omission of the annual inspection due in 1898 was sanctioned by the Education Department and the annual Total Grant for the school was recorded as £61-2-0, Reductions £1-19-6, leaving £59-2-6. However, a fee grant of £6-0-0 resulted in £65-2-6 being payable to the school.

While excellent progress was made with the education of children with normal abilities, it was impossible for every child with learning difficulties to be accommodated. Thus, in 1888, among several new pupils, was an eight year old boy who could *'only make sounds instead of talking'*, being *'very deficient in intellect'*. He gave *'a great deal of trouble at school, in destroying things...'* and after three weeks he was assessed by Rev Stanton, who considered him to be *'far too deficient in intellect to be allowed to remain at school'*, so he was taken off the registers.

A particular problem, particularly for rural schools, was that each autumn term there was a turnover of pupils because at Michaelmas farm labourers and other workers often moved away, having been hired at the Michaelmas fairs ('Mops') to work for farmers in other parishes. Conversely there was an influx of new pupils, often with inferior education. In 1890 Mrs Alcock wrote that the new pupils were very backward in their standard work and that this would have a detrimental effect on the forthcoming examination results (and consequently on the government grants), some as old as 7 years *'hardly knowing a letter or a figure'* and *'nearly all are children from off the hills'*.

The Codes for grants of 1893 and 1896 added more subjects to the curriculum and teachers were encouraged to plan class visits to museums, art galleries and historic buildings. Towards the end of the 19th century school games, physical exercises and military drill were also encouraged [1].

Expansion of the Curriculum at Didbrook School

In 1890 weekly drawing classes for the boys, given by a visiting teacher, were introduced and in 1898 the girls began to attend cooking courses at Toddington.

In 1908 Lady Elcho invited the children to tea and a performance in the grounds of Stanway House of 'As you like it' by the Oxford Dramatic Society. Also the children went by train to Cheltenham to watch the Gloucestershire pageant (Rev Stanton provided the rail tickets) and the following week they wrote about the various episodes in the pageant. Drama performances were also undertaken from time to time by the children, especially to mark local or national events.

Girl pupils in costume outside Didbrook School circa 1916-18.   Judy and Mary Horlick are the 6th and 2nd pupils from the right.

As well as providing religious education, the local clergy contributed to the curriculum in several ways. Thus in 1907 Rev Allen, curate at Didbrook Church, celebrated Empire Day by giving the children a talk about the great men who had built up the Empire, and he read to them about the relief of Lucknow. In 1909 his successor, Rev J C Farr, gave them an address and the Day was celebrated by giving a flag to each child, singing the National Anthem, recitations by the children, and the Infants' Action Songs. Also, In December 1907 Rev Farr gave the children a Magic Lantern entertainment on Australian Bush life.

In February 1912 Mr Horace Horlick started classes for the boys in wood-carving, using pen-knives, and in 1917 permission was obtained from Gloucester Education Committee to include gardening within their school work. The butcher, Mr Herbert Archer, gave a piece of ground in the allotment opposite the school for the children to cultivate. Gardening became an official part of the curriculum for boys and girls and in 1926 at the Horticultural Show at Toddington four Didbrook pupils won prizes for their work. Gardening classes, mostly on growing vegetables for boys and growing flowers for girls, were continued with some interruptions until 1933, when they ceased because of the small number of boys attending the school then. The current head mistress's husband, Mr Colin Holdsworth, thereafter had the garden for his own use and so that vegetables might continue to be provided for the school dinners. Instruction on gardening was resumed in 1944, when Mr King of Stanton was engaged as Gardening Instructor for four hours a week.

On April 14th 1927 the school closed at 11.45 for the midday recess, 'so that the Meet of Hounds nearbye could be witnessed'. There were a number of subsequent occasions when the then head (Mr Gay) permitted this particular addition to the curriculum! He also arranged on September 30th for some of the older children to go to the Headmaster's House to listen to the play 'Abraham Lincoln' relayed for school children by the BBC.

Scholarships

Balfour's Education Act (1902) had several important effects [2]. It brought all voluntary and board schools under municipal control and set up an organised system of elementary (limited to age less than 16 years), secondary and technical education. It also replaced the School Boards and Attendance Committees by Local Education Authorities, extended the scholarship system so that many more poor scholars could obtain secondary education, and improved teacher training. Some aspects of this Act were not fully implemented until after WWII, but from the 1920s it greatly benefited the number of Didbrook School's pupils who were able to progress to Grammar schools (and by then they could travel to them easily, by rail from Toddington Station or Hailes Halt). Hitherto, only those pupils who could afford the fees and who had their own transport could attend them.

Thus, on February 15th 1922 Mr Maybury received a circular from the Education Committee about Free Places and Scholarships available at the Grammar School that year; the parents of 3 pupils asked for their children to be allowed to enter the scholarship examinations, but unfortunately none was successful, nor were Charles Hughes and Gladys Jones, who sat the examination in 1923. However, in 1924 Charles Hughes' parents were persuaded to allow him to sit the examination again, and he was granted a place at Cheltenham Grammar School as a Scholarship student. He was probably the first pupil of Didbrook School to win such an award, and he took up his place in September 1924. In July 1926 Gladys Jones passed the Scholarship examination for the

Technical College at Cheltenham, also probably the first pupil from Didbrook School so to do.

A list of pupils who obtained places at local grammar schools, the Technical College and other schools is shown in Table 6. The boys who attended Winchcombe Grammar School (which closed around 1907) would have been fee-paying, but even after scholarships were introduced, for some children these paid only a part of the cost of the fees, the remainder having to be met by the child's family. For example, in July 1929 Alec Bowles and Denis Wright were told that they may attend the Technical School at a reduced fee of £1 12s 6d per term.

Probably to assist children hoping to progress to secondary schools, in 1923 books were obtained for the PNEU (Parents' National Education Union, of Ambleside) Scheme. This provided a syllabus for primary schools and also examinations, supervised by HMIs, to test pupils on the work that they studied.

With Mrs Holdsworth's appointment as Headmistress in 1929 the number and variety of educational excursions increased markedly, some of which are described in Chapter 3. She also continued to arrange for the children to listen to the BBC broadcasts for schools, at her own home until she was able to buy a 'wireless' for the school. Unfortunately most of the excursions had to be forfeited during WW II, but they were resumed afterwards.

Didbrook School's transition to become a Primary School

The Hadow Report of 1926 [2] recommended separation of Elementary (Primary) from Secondary Schools, and the Spens Report of 1938 [3] envisaged three forms of secondary education, suited to the child's abilities: Grammar, Technical High and Secondary Modern. The 1936 Education Act aimed to raise the school leaving age to 15 years by 1939 [4]. While the new secondary schools were opened in many areas, WW II delayed full implementation of these proposals, which were re-iterated in the 1944 and 1948 Education Acts [5, 6].

The school leaving age was eventually raised to 15 years in 1947. However, in some parts of the UK, separation of primary from secondary education necessitated building new schools and it was not fully realised in the Winchcombe area until Winchcombe Secondary Modern School opened in 1952. So, at Didbrook, Mrs Holdsworth and Miss Last

Table 6.   **DIDBROOK SCHOOL**

Pupils who gained Scholarships, Grammar School or College places

Year	Name	Placement/Scholarship/Award
1882	Frank Horlick	Winchcombe Grammar School (WGS)
	James Stanley	WGS
1884	Edward Horlick	WGS
1885	Leigh James	WGS
1886	George Minchins	WGS
1893	William Horlick	WGS
1909	Alwyn Scarlett	Cheltenham Grammar School (CGS)
1924	Charles Hughes	CGS (scholarship)
1926	Gladys Jones	Cheltenham Technical College(CTS) (scholarship)
1927	Vernon Horlick	CGS (scholarship)
	Charles Ballinger	CGS (scholarship)
	Jessica (Jess) Edmonds	Pate's Grammar School for Girls (PGSG)
	Leslie Archer	CTS (scholarship)
	Sydney Nash	CTS (scholarship)
	Marjorie Archer	PGSG (scholarship)
1928	Olga Jones	CTS (scholarship)
1929	Dorothy Joan Millward	PGSG (scholarship)
	Amy Wyniatt	PGSG (scholarship)
	Alec Bowles	CTS (scholarship)
	Denis Wright	CTS (scholarship)
1930	Winifred Cox	PGSG (scholarship)
	Eva Parnell	PGSG (scholarship)
	John Harrison	Chipping Campden Grammar School
	Marjorie Harrison	Chipping Campden Grammar School
	Frank Hughes	CGS (scholarship)
1931	Laurence Bolton	CGS (scholarship)
	Oswald Culverwell	CGS
1932	Kathleen Wyniatt	Glos College of Domestic Science (GCDS)
	Gladys Nash	PGSG (scholarship)
1933	Marion Roberts	PGSG (scholarship)
1934	Elia Joan Horlick	CTS (scholarship)
	Gwendoline Cox	CTS (scholarship)
1935	Peter Stanford	CGS (scholarship)
1936	Doris Edmonds	GCDS (scholarship)
	Frederick Archer	CGS (scholarship)
	Barbara Lane	PGSG (scholarship)
	Leslie Doughty	CTS (scholarship)
1937	Rose Cox	PGSG (scholarship)
	Geoffrey Righton	CGS(scholarship)
	Clarence Walter Turner	CTS
1938	Lancelot Jones	CGS (scholarship)
1939	Peggy Ingles	CTS (scholarship)

	Marjorie Doughty	PGSG (scholarship)
1940	Elizabeth Wright	PGSG (scholarship)
1941	Irene Baker	PGSG (scholarship)
	John Cox	CGS (scholarship)
	Harold Righton	CTS
	Douglas Reed	CTS (now Cheltenham Technical College?)
1942	Gordon Fuller (evacuee)	Technical College in Birmingham (scholarship)
	Robert Aird (evacuee)	CGS (scholarship)
	Marjorie Righton	PGSG (scholarship)
	Mildred Gurton	PGSG (scholarship). Went to Central School, Chelt.
1944	Jacqueline Budden	PGSG (scholarship)
	Geoffrey Bowles	CGS (scholarship)
	Victor Vickery (evacuee)	Passed Birmingham Special Place examination
1946	Eric Righton	CGS
	Lionel Glyn Wright	CGS (scholarship)
	Wendy Sadler	PGSG (scholarship)
1950	Jillian Rose Mann	PGSG (scholarship)
	Florence Wakefield	PGSG (scholarship)
	Margaret Ingles	Tewkesbury High School for Girls(THS) (scholarship)
1951	Patrick Newman	CGS (scholarship)
	Ann Sadler	PGSG (scholarship)
1952	David Risborough	Tewkesbury Grammar School (TGS) (scholarship)
	Margaret Mann	THS (scholarship)
	Susan Mann	THS (scholarship)
	Pauline Whitcombe	THS (scholarship)
1957	Michael Boardman	THS(scholarship)
	Margaret Hardiman	THS (scholarship), went to Northleach Grammar Sch?
1958	Roger Archer	TGS (scholarship)
1963	David Groom	TGS
1964	Claire Smith	PGSG (scholarship)
1966	Ian Hayward	CTS
1968	Jane Hayward	CTS
1969	Teresa Davis	Convent School, Cheltenham
1972	Robert Harris	CGS
1977	Philip Andrews	CGS (scholarship)
	Gillian Hayward	PGSG
	Anna Haynes	Chipping Campden GS
	Gareth Thomas	CGS
1978	Sarah Andrews	Convent School, Cheltenham
1979	Geraint Thomas	CGS
1980	Joanne Foley	PGSG (scholarship)
	Joe Langston	Chipping Campden GS
1980	Jacqueline Hayward	PGSG
1985	Nicholas Smith	Rendcombe College
1994	Drew Leich	Pate's Grammar School (PGS)
1997	Robert Gwynn-Jones	PGS

	Jonathan Titchin	Exeter Cathedral Choral School
2005	Phoebe Harding	High School for Girls, Gloucester
2008	Kate Harding	Ditto

This table includes only the children who moved directly from Didbrook School to the named schools and colleges, and it could be incomplete. There were additional children (particularly from the 1950s) who won places to them via other schools. For example, Anne and Elizabeth Holmes went from Didbrook School to Winchcombe Secondary Modern School and then to Cheltenham Technical School.

Mrs Alcock seated on a bench in middle age. How proud she would have been
that pupils of her beloved school achieved so much!
(Photograph provided by Mrs Elizabeth Brett)

continued to provide education for children ranging in age from 5 to 15 years until then.

An unfortunate but thankfully short effect of Didbrook School becoming a primary school was a fall in its roll to only 25 pupils. Consequently, in January 1953 Miss Last was transferred to Toddington School for six months, leaving Mrs Holdsworth teaching single-handedly until the roll increased.

The curriculum was adjusted to suit the younger age profile of the pupils so, for example, in July 1953 Mrs Holdsworth took 12 junior children to the First North Cotswold Schools' Music Festival at Cheltenham. In 1954 percussion instruments were obtained for a percussion band, and in 1957 the junior class participated in the annual Schools' Music Festival at Bishop's Cleeve.

Mrs Holdsworth's successor, Miss Southerden, introduced the new less structured approach to education, particularly to encourage learning by self-expression and discovery, rather than by rote, as advocated in the Plowden Report of 1967 [7]. She enacted some of its other recommendations too, such as the abolition of corporal punishment in schools. She also encouraged drama and music and arranged further educational visits, mostly to local venues. Thus, in 1961 she or her assistant took the children to Didbrook Fields Farm (where they saw the milking parlour, piggeries and machine sheds), in 1965 to Bristol Zoo, in 1966 to Cheltenham Museum and Art Gallery, in 1967 to Hailes Abbey, Winchcombe Potteries and a lecture at Cheltenham about the Cotswold wool trade, in 1968 to Stanway House and its Tithe Barn to study their architecture and in 1970 to the Cotswold Wild Life Park.

The next two head teachers, Ieuan Lewis and David Sanders, also expanded the curriculum, particularly by encouraging sport. Football was introduced in 1971 and Mr Lewis formed a team that competed against local schools. They lost their first match, against Brook School, Wordsley 17- 0, but enjoyed the game and had greater success in subsequent matches. Instruction in cycling, with proficiency tests, was started by PC Hutson in 1972 and this training was taken over in 1978 by PC David Collins, who continued to do it for most of the next 30 years.

In April 1972 Mr Lewis arranged for pupils to go to Winchcombe Junior School's swimming pool and on June 23rd that year he also held the school's first Annual Sports Day. Six days later he held an Open Day at

Didbrook School's team, which were joint winners of the Area Rounders tournament at Stanway Cricket ground on July 1st 1987:

Front row:
Samantha Turpitt, Donna Andrews, Alice Potterton, Angela Pitt,
Sarah Collins, Rachel Beard

Back row:
Daniel Roberts, Stuart Beard, Scott Walford, Adam Hensley, Kevin Harris,
Paul Burrows

Standing behind them:
Mr David Sanders

which there were competitions for wild flower arranging and miniature gardens, and prizes were given for these competitions and for school work, including prizes for the boy and girl who had made the greatest all round progress during the year. In the autumn, at Rev Bidlake's request, the children took part in the Harvest Festival at Didbrook Church, and in November the children and staff saw Beauty and the Beast at the Everyman Theatre.

Collaboration with other local primary schools (in Winchcombe, Gretton, Alderton, Guiting Power, Toddington, Dumbleton and Ashton) was increased, to allow regular sports competitions, swimming instruction and galas, and cross country running matches. In 1978 Didbrook School won the shield at the Area Village School Sports Day held in Winchcombe for seven local Schools and they had similar success in 1987 at the Annual Rounders tournament, which was held at Stanway Cricket Field.

Christmas Play, 1988 'The Punctuation Party'

Front row: unknown, Damon Walford, Martin Hill, Peter Green, Jennifer Higgins, Lizzie Potterton, Stephanie Keogh-Golisch Visible standing behind: Donna Andrews, Becky Foley, Daniel Fisher, Kelly Law

Both local and more distant educational visits continued as well as theatre trips and expeditions to the Three Counties Agricultural Shows. In 1986 eight juniors joined children from Mitton Manor and Twyning Primary Schools on an educational week in the Isle of Wight, in 1987 ten children were taken to York for a week (see chapter 3) and in 1988 children and staff went on a 3 day residential course at the Wilderness Centre, Micheldean. Additional sports, such as hockey and cricket, were introduced and in 1984 recorder lessons were started. In December 1988 the children performed a Christmas Play, 'The Punctuation Party'. Mr Sanders wrote '*Unfortunately we were without 2 full stops and a colon, who were down with 'flu, but we coped without them*'.

Modernising the School and Changes to Education

Didbrook School had access to radio broadcasts from the late 1920s, and its relative isolation was eased further by the installation of a telephone and a tape recorder in 1971 and a black and white television set in 1973. Mr Sanders collected the school's first computer on September 21st 1983 and by November the children were starting to use this. Gradually many other computers were bought and in 2003 the Friends of Didbrook School (FODS) raised money to provide a widescreen television with video player and DVD.

The Education Reform Act of 1988 [8] included a new National Curriculum, to start in September 1989, the introduction of 'Key Stages', by the end of each of which (at 7, 11 and 14 years of age) certain educational objectives were to be achieved, and league tables were established which would publish and compare the examination results of schools. Local Management of Schools (LMS), which handed over financial control from Local Authorities to head teachers and governors of schools, was also included in the Act and was phased in over the next few years.

On January 18th 1989 Mr Sanders attended the first of many parts of a course on the new curriculum for Head Teachers, and the other teachers also undertook courses. The staff of the small school at Didbrook, (two full-time, one part-time and a few other part-timers providing sessions covering music, special needs, PE etc) found their extra training and implementing the new curriculum stressful. This was partly due to the fact that in small schools the classes had to contain mixed age groups. Mr Sanders recorded generally low morale at a meeting of head teachers in Cheltenham in November 1989, and that the autumn term was exhausting. The Log Book confirms that the time spent on training the teaching staff remained high in subsequent years and that in 1990 the Governors also had to go on extra courses to help them deal with '*the mountain of paper that now afflicts us*'.

Over time the government made extra money available to assist small schools to work together in 'clusters' on local projects. Thus Didbrook, Toddington, Oak Hill (Alderton with Dumbleton) and Gretton Schools began to share resources and expertise. They secured funding for specialist teachers to assist in curriculum areas such as technology and music and worked with Winchcombe School, using it as a base for workshops, theatre groups and other activities.

The SATS (Standard Attainment Tests) to evaluate the progress of children following the National Curriculum were started in April 1991, and in February 1993 two of the County's Inspectors inspected the school, following a changeover in the national inspections system from HMI to OFSTED.

The further plethora of legislation and governmental recommendations had less major consequences for primary schools than did the 1988 Reform Act. They included the Education Acts of 1993 [9] and 2001 [10] which incorporated, among other matters, the provision for children with special educational needs at mainstream schools; ever since 1978 Didbrook School had had part-time staff trained to work with such children (to allow the school to cope with all except the very severely disabled) and the possibility of extra provision was welcomed. The 1993 Act also stated that at maintained primary schools sex education would remain discretionary and parents would have a right to withdraw their children from all or part of the sex education offered. In 1999 written Home-School Agreements, signed by parents, and a daily Literacy Hour, which aimed to improve the reading and writing abilities of pupils, were introduced. The Education Act of 1996 [11] confirmed the school leaving age to be 16 years.

Broadening the Curriculum

In parallel with implementing the various legislative changes the staff, assisted by parents and other volunteers, continued to extend the curriculum, in particular by increasing the educational visits, sport and musical activities. Thus, in 1989 children were taken to Ironbridge, in 1990 for three days to the Wilderness Centre in the Forest of Dean, in 1991

Abseiling on the Isle of Wight, 1991

Archery on the Isle of Wight, 1991

for a week to the Isle of Wight, in 1992 for a week to Cornwall and in 1994 to France. Further trips included in 1997 the Butterfly Centre at Stratford upon Avon and the Corinium museum at Cirencester, in 1998 Slimbridge Wildfowl Trust and four days at Kingswood Centre in Norfolk, and in 1998 and 1999 residential courses on the Isle of Wight. Similar trips continued in the 2000s, including residential visits to Bethany House (a PGL outdoor activities centre in Surrey) in 2000 and 2001, to Kingswood Centre Norfolk in 2003 and to Hillcrest adventure centre in the Wye Valley in 2006.

Musical activities made available during the 1990s and 2000s included taking part in 'The Magic Flute' at Stanway Tithe Barn in 1991, playing recorder, guitar, keyboard, trumpet, violin, cello, singing 'Hosanna Rock' at Didbrook Church and choral singing lessons with Mr Malcolm Foster.

The sports activities were increased by adding netball, rounders, cricket, tag rugby and athletics to the previous repertoire. From the mid-2000s Mr Darren Hayling provided regular sports coaching on a voluntary basis and organised matches with other small schools in the Winchcombe area.

Throughout its history, the staff with the pupils and their parents, supported many local and national events in the Church and community and also many charitable causes, as well as fundraising to enhance the school's curriculum. In the 21st century the school supported a number of humanitarian causes aiming to relieve disasters across the world, such as the Somalia Appeal in 2002.

Sports Day on the School playing field, 2004. Hailes Wood is in the distance. (JRM) Left to right: Liam Mustoe, Joe White, unknown

*Pancake race past Didbrook Church, 1989:
Left to right: Donna Andrews, Stuart Beard, Benjy Turpitt, Pippa Harvey,
Matthew Greenhalf, Daniel Roberts, Sam Gregory and behind them: Mr
David Sanders (Headmaster)*

Nativity Play at Didbrook Church, 1989
Left to right: unknown, Martin Beard, unknown, Rachel Bolton,
unknown, unknown, Peter Green

At Hayles Fruit Farm, summer 1990:
Front row: Darren Boulton, Georgina Hall, Kelly Law, Joanna Cooper, Toby
Shaw, Donna Andrews, Sarah Hill, unknown, Stephanie Keogh-Golisch
Back row: Emily Hill, Rachel Bolton, David Williams, Zoe Strickland,
Jennifer Higgins, Lizzie Potterton, Joanna Higgins, Martin Beard,
Daniel Roberts, Peter Green, Tim Williams, Richard Hall, Micko Uedelhoven,
Colin Bostock, Anthony Johns, unknown

Lizzie Potterton, Colin Bostock and Ashley Mitchell preparing vegetables for a Harvest supper to raise money for the Somalia Appeal in 2002

Mrs Hilda Archer, Mrs Francoise Horlick, Mrs Amy Wright and Mrs Eileen Phillips at the Harvest supper for the Somalia Appeal, 2002

In 2006 the headmaster, Mr Ogden, obtained a considerable EU grant, to fund the Comenius Project for the 3 years 2006-9. This set up links between Didbrook School and schools in Finland (Tampere) and France (Liffré, near Rennes). The children exchanged Christmas messages in 2006 and Mr Ogden was made very welcome when he visited Tampere in January 2007 and February 2008, and Liffré in March 2007. On his return he taught both the Infants and Juniors about Finland and France. Also, teachers from the French school visited Didbrook in June 2007 and worked with the Infants and Juniors. Pen pals were established with children from the French school. The pupils from the three schools together wrote an illustrated 'folk tale'. The Project led to the school being awarded 'International School' (Intermediate) status by the British Council.

Achievements of Some Former Pupils

Showing how education at Didbrook School has benefited its pupils should ideally be done by describing the achievements of all its former pupils. To obtain this information on everyone is difficult, but an impression can be gained by briefly describing the careers of a few.

Jack Hughes, the eldest son of Joseph Hughes, a gardener at Stanway House, and his wife, Anne, trained as a gardener at Stanway House, Watford and Sandringham Palace. He then became Head Gardener at Bristol Zoo. Their second son Charles was, in 1924, probably he first pupil of Didbrook School to win a scholarship to attend Cheltenham Grammar School. He then trained as a pharmacist in London and worked in several Boots' stores, before becoming manager of their shop in Cheltenham High Street. Their third son Bert (Albert) worked first at Purton's Grocery shop at Toddington, delivering groceries to many of the big houses in the area, and then in a similar shop in Cranford village, near London Heathrow Airport. After active service in WW II and four years in a prisoner of war camp in Germany, he married and set up his own grocery business at Westbury on Trym, near Bristol. The Hughes' fourth son, Frank, like his brother, Charles, won a scholarship to Cheltenham Grammar School and trained as a pharmacist with Boots in Nottingham. He went into partnership with another Mr Hughes (no relation) to buy a chemists shop in Churchdown, Cheltenham, and returned to Stanway to live. There he became a respected member of the community as Clerk to the Governors of Didbrook School, Parish Councillor, a principal organiser of the annual Stanway Flower Show and a staunch church-goer.

The first girl recorded to gain a scholarship to Pate's Grammar School for Girls from Didbrook School was Jessica Edmonds, a daughter of the Head Gamekeeper on Stanway Estate, Albert ('Gaffer') Edmonds. She became a teacher and spent most of her life teaching at Willersey School. Subsequently several other pupils also became school teachers, including Marjorie Righton, Margaret Ingles and Margaret Mann.

Geoffrey Righton, eldest son of Austen Righton, who farmed Glebe Farm at Wood Stanway, may have been the first pupil of Didbrook School to go from Cheltenham Grammar School to university; he studied agriculture at Reading and became the manager and subsequently a director of Stokes Bomford Farms, near Evesham. Others who progressed to university degrees via the local Grammar Schools included Glyn Wright (electrical engineering at Sheffield; became a partner in a firm making industrial heat treatment equipment in Cheltenham), Jillian Mann (medicine at London; became consultant in Paediatric Oncology at Birmingham Children's Hospital), Geraint Thomas (social administration at London, became a social worker in mental health in Bristol) and Gareth Thomas (history at Durham University, became a partner in a law firm in Hong Kong).

Soon after leaving Cheltenham Grammar School, Geoffrey Bowles was called up and joined the RAF. He won a scholarship to the RAF College at Cranwell, and progressed to become Commanding Officer of 99 Squadron at Brize Norton. For a while he served with the Queen's Flight and in 1972 he was awarded the Queen's Commendation for Valuable Services in the Air. He retired after 37 years in the RAF with the rank of Wing Commander, but unfortunately died soon afterwards, in 1991.

Philip Andrews, after farming experience at Didbrook, Norfolk, Harper Adams College and abroad, has worked since 1991 as a civil servant in London, specialising on rural affairs with DEFRA, as a junior assistant to two of Tony Blair's specials advisors in 10 Downing Street and doing projects for the Department of Energy and Climate Change. Susan Mann also went into farming, with her husband John Firkins, and they now have a fruit farm near Worcester.

Many former pupils had or have, businesses in Stanway Parish or nearby villages, including Lesley Archer (village butcher) and his son Roger (cabinet maker at Gordon Russell's), Eva Turpitt née Purnell (postmistress), Wendy Butler née Sadler (bed and breakfast) and her sisters Ann Tilley and Jill Carenza (riding schools), Neil Grimmett (builder) and Philip Mann (following further education at Dean Close School and Seale Hayne Agricultural College) took over W Mann and Sons and farms land at Didbrook, Stanway, Coscombe, Taddington and Cutsdean.

SOURCES

1.   Curtis SJ. History of Education in Great Britain, 7th Edition, University Tutorial Press, London, 1967
2.   Hadow WH. The Education of the Adolescent. Report to the Board of Education. HMSO, London, 1926
3.   Spens W. Report of the consultative committee on secondary education with special reference in grammar schools and technical high schools. Report to the Board of Education. HMSO, London,1938
4.   Education Act, 1936
5.   Education Act (Butler) 1944
6.   Education (Miscellaneous Provisions) Act 1948
7.   The Plowden Report 1967. Children and their Primary Schools. A Report of the Central Advisory Council for Education (England). HMSO, London, 1967
8.   Education Reform Act 1988
9.   Education Act 1993
10.   Education Act 2001
11.   Education Act 1996

Chapter 6.
DIDBROOK SCHOOL IN WARTIME

I have had playmates, I have had companions,
In my days of childhood, in my joyful schooldays
Ah, all are gone, the old familiar faces.

Charles Lamb (1775-1834) The Old Familiar Faces

The Second Boer War (1899-1902)

The first mention of war in the Log books was in February 1900, when Mrs Alcock recorded that nearly all the girls were knitting pairs of socks to be sent to soldiers in South Africa who were fighting in the second Boer War. Also, the Rector's daughter, Miss Ethel Stanton, visited and spoke to the children about a children's penny fund for building a convalescent home for sailors and soldiers. The children were taught a new patriotic song '*The dear old flag of England*' and in 1901 their geography lessons included learning about '*British Possessions*' in Canada, the West Indies, Central and South America, Australia, Tasmania and New Zealand. While few families appeared to be personally involved with the Boer War, in July 1902 John Dunford spent some time away from school because he had gone '*to meet his father, a reservist from South Africa*'. Among other local men who were serving in the armed forces then was Mrs Alcock's son, AG Alcock of the Royal Engineers Brompton Barracks, Chatham. In one week of December 1902 he '*gave the children exercise in Military drill each day*' and there were a number of subsequent occasions when he (or other local soldiers) did this.

The First World War (1914-1918)

This war had a much greater impact on the school. War with Germany broke out during the summer holidays of 1914 and the children returned to school on September 7th. During the first week of term Lady Elcho visited and asked them to invite their mothers to meet at Stanway, with a view to doing needlework and knitting for the soldiers and sailors. By October some of the schoolgirls had also made socks and scarves for them.

Mrs Alcock included information about the war in lessons and in September 1914 the children wrote on the loss of three ships in the North Sea, took '*sea shells*' as their nature study and sang '*Ye mariners of England*'. In October their lessons included having articles read to them about the war, finding the places involved on maps and writing a composition on the fall of Antwerp and the German occupation. The children received a special prayer from the Bishop of Gloucester and learnt 'The land of my Fathers'. In November they were shown pictures of the war and wrote about the battleship HMS Bulwark going down off Sheerness following an explosion.

During the first week of 1915, the children again saw pictures and read papers on the war and noted the Russian victory over the Turks in the Caucasus. They brought in eggs from their homes to be sent to the wounded in the Red Cross Hospital. Later in January they wrote on the naval battle in the North and the sinking of the German ship, the Blucher. In February they had extracts from daily papers on the war and the Blockade of the English coasts read to them.

In March the Upper Standard children did compositions on the ships forcing the passage of the Dardanelles, sang 'The Pilot' from the Ancient Mariner and studied the geography of the Balkan Peninsula, with the Dardanelles. By April they were able to sing the French, Belgian and Russian National anthems. They wrote about the sinking of the Lusitania, which was torpedoed by the Germans, saw war pictures, read extracts from the newspapers, and talked about HMS Triumph being torpedoed in the Dardanelles and a ship blown up at Sheerness. They looked up Trentino in the Tyrol and noted the position of Italy in the war and 'read picture post cards from soldiers at the front who were boys at this school'. In July the school was visited by Miss Wedgwood from Stanton accompanied by a Belgian lady who spoke to the children about the condition of Belgium through the war. The children sang the Belgian National Anthem and gave the lady a Belgian Flag kettle holder worked by them. In January 1916 the Upper Standard girls knitted socks for the soldiers and the following month the children wrote letters on the Zeppelin air raid on the Midland Counties which occurred on the night of February 1st.

The 'Home Front'

The war led to many difficulties on the 'Home Front'. As early as February 1915 Rev Allen received from the County Education Officer a circular about the increasing cost and scarcity of coal. Economies were therefore necessary and, as well as using wood when available instead of coal, the school hours were reduced to the minimum allowed of 2 hours in the morning and 2 in the afternoon; morning school was to end at 11.45 and afternoon school to begin at 12.45 and end at 2.50. Despite these measures, the school was closed from December 17th to January 10th 1916 because of the expense and shortage of coal.

The schoolchildren themselves assisted in the war effort. For example, in September 1917 notice was received from Gloucestershire Education Committee that half holidays were to be given to the children to allow them to pick blackberries for the Army and Navy. On September 17th 62 lbs were picked and the whole of the following day was also devoted to picking, and on September 19th 93 lbs were sent from Winchcombe station to factories. After another two days picking, a further 134 lbs of blackberries were sent off on September 26th.

Many men from the villages served in the armed forces during the war, with the result that some families lost their breadwinners, at least for the duration of the war. For example, in November 1915 Mrs Chaplin asked for her son Alfred, who was aged 13, to be released from school to work in the fruit plantation at Hailes, because her husband was in delicate health and her other three boys had all gone to the war. Mrs Alcock agreed to this request.

Local Heroes

On September 20th 1915 Mrs Lanchbury asked permission for her children to go to the station with their father, who was going abroad with the 3rd Gloucesters, and in October Bertie Wynniatt stayed at home with his mother for a day because his brother, Pte Frank C Wynniatt, a former pupil of the school, had been killed in action in France.

Following Mrs Alcock's retirement at the end of 1915, records about what happened to the many former pupils who served in the armed forces during the war are sparse. Perhaps her successors found the details too painful to record. Altogether, including Frank Wyniatt and Wilfred Lanchbury (possibly the man referred to above whose children saw him off to war), 17 men from Didbrook parish were killed. Among these were Mrs Alcock's son, Alfred, who died in the Battle of the Somme in 1916 and Pte William Edgar Holmes, who died at Cattenières on the 9th October, 1918, and was awarded the Victoria Cross.

Table 7 records all the 17 men of Didbrook Parish who died in the war and also the 12 men of Stanway who were killed [1]. In addition, John James, who was born at Hailes, died in the Battle of the Somme. Such large losses of men from these small villages must have had a considerable impact.

Table 7.   **WAR MEMORIALS**

MEMORIALS IN DIDBROOK CHURCH

1914-1918
Lieut Alfred Alcock, 1st Glos Regt
Lieut John C Hutchinson, 6th East Surrey Regt
Pte Harry C Doughty, 2/4 R Berks
Pte Wilfred Simpson, R Marine L Inf
Corpl Denis F Wright, 7th Glos Regt
Pte Edgar F Jones, 2nd Ryl Worc Regt
Pte Frank C Wynniatt, 10th Glos Regt
Pte Wilfred Lanchbury, 8th Glos Regt
Pte William C Buttell, 10th Linc Regt
Pte Arthur Clements, 1st Glos Regt
Sapr Charles Simpson, 116th Rail Co. R.E.
Pte Arthur L Gissing, 20th Hussars
Pte John Simpson, 7th Glos Regt
Pte Edward J Innes, 2nd Glos Regt,
Pte Thomas Simpson, 10th Glos Regt
Pte Herbert Minchin, 10th Glos Regt
Pte Will. Edgar Holmes, Gren Guards, VC

1939-1945
Sergt William Grove Spencer RAFVR

MEMORIALS IN STANWAY CHURCH

1914-1918
Alfred Henry Buggins
Frank Buggins
Henry Charles Thombs
Hubert Thombs
Ernest James Townsend
William James Ewington
Francis Lane
Hugo Francis Charteris, Lord Elcho
Yvo Alan Charteris
Charles Richard
Gerald Mitchell
Frederick Starkey

1939-1945
Lawrence John Samuel Bolton
Reginald Victor Turpitt

WAR MEMORIAL AT STANWAY CROSSROADS
This is engraved 'Men of Stanway' and records only the men lost in the First World War (as in Stanway Church, but William James Ewington is not included, possibly because he did not live in Stanway).

The War Memorial at Stanway, which was dedicated by the Lord Bishop of Gloucester on October 30th, 1920 (JRM).

Pte William Edgar Holmes, VC
(photograph provided by Mr Alan Vickers).

After the war

After the end of the war, Armistice Day was celebrated at the school each year. For example on November 11th 1920, the children were addressed and then sang 'O God our help in ages past' and at 11 am two minutes silence was observed. On November 11th 1929 the school attended Didbrook Church to observe the two minutes silence and before going there Mrs Holdsworth gave a short talk *'on our debt to the men who fought, and our need to support the League of Nations to promote peace.'*

On June 26th 1956 Mrs Holdsworth took the children into Didbrook Church to see the wall plaque commemorating Pte William Edgar Holmes VC, late 2nd battalion, Grenadier Guards, an old boy of the school. His 90 years old father was that week attending the Centenary Celebrations in London, at the Queen's invitation. Edgar's citation read: 'For most conspicuous bravery and devotion to duty at Cattenieres on the 9th October, 1918. Pte Holmes carried two men under the most intense fire, and, while he was attending to a third case, he was severely wounded. In spite of this, he continued to carry wounded, and was shortly afterwards again wounded, with fatal results. By his self-sacrifice and disregard of danger he was the means of saving the lives of several of his comrades' [2]. Edgar was awarded the Victoria Cross posthumously.

The Second World War (1939-1945)

The likelihood of another war was heralded by a visit in June 1938 from Lt Col Knight (Chairman of Managers) about Air Raid Precautions and on October 6th the school closed early to allow the room to be used *'for ARP fitting of gas masks'*.

On January 30th 1939 Mrs Holdsworth attended the quarterly meeting of the Women's Voluntary Services for Air Raid Precautions in the Shire Hall, Gloucester (she attended subsequent meetings as the representative of the Gloucestershire County National Union of Teachers). Also, in May Miss Last started to attend Nursing lectures arranged in connection with the National Defence plans, and an HMV Wireless set was installed in the school, paid for from School Funds.

Evacuees

War broke out on September 1st, 1939 and the autumn term started a few days late. This was because the schoolroom had been needed as an Evacuation centre for the reception of mothers and babies from

Birmingham. When the school re-opened on September 11th, 7 evacuees were enrolled, 6 from Birmingham and one from London, who was evacuated to live with her aunt in Didbrook.

On March 1st 1940 Miss Fairhead, Head Teacher of Redhill Infants and Junior School, Hay Mills, Birmingham, called to discuss the proposed evacuation of children from her school to Didbrook and on March 28th Mr Davis, the Birmingham teacher appointed to accompany them, spent the afternoon at Didbrook School. On April 4th 17 children from the Birmingham area were evacuated and enrolled at Didbrook School, increasing its roll to 64. Mr Wyndham H Davies was appointed by the Birmingham Education Committee to assist at Didbrook School and Mr S Wood was the Chief Billeting Officer who allocated the children to homes in the area. Subsequently, other children from Birmingham, Essex, Dagenham, London, Eastbourne, Ramsgate and Liverpool were received, bringing the total number of children of school age who were evacuated into the villages and became pupils at Didbrook School to at least 70. Table 8 shows the names of the evacuees and their hosts [3, 4].

From March 3rd 1941 27 senior boys and girls were taught by Mr Davies in the Memorial (Village) Hall at Stanway, to relieve the overcrowding in Didbrook School. However, on August 12th 1941 Mr Davies left, having been called up for duty in the RAF, and he was replaced in September by Mrs Daisy Beatrice Philpott.

On May 13th 1941 the Lord Mayor and Lady Mayoress of Birmingham (Col Wilfrid and Mrs Martineau) visited the school, with the school managers also present, and on July 31st 'Miss Fairhead, Head Teacher of Redhill Junior School, Haymills, Birmingham, visited her children evacuated here today. She said she was greatly impressed by the improvement in health and physique and the evidence of the care of the foster parents'.

During March 1944 both Mrs Philpott and Mrs Holdsworth visited Red Hill Infants and Junior School, Hay Mills, Birmingham to report on their care of evacuees from that school; Mrs Holdsworth also visited Cromwell Street Infants and Junior School in Birmingham. On April 5th Mrs Philpott relinquished her duties at Didbrook (and presumably returned to Birmingham).

Table 8.

EVACUEES AT DIDBROOK SCHOOL

Name	Date of birth	Stayed with	Date arrived	Date left	Last School
John Blackburn	18.12.32	Mrs Archer, Didbrook	11.9.39	15.9.39	Little Green Lane, B'ham
*Joyce Markham	11.1.31	Mrs Lively, Didbrook	11.9.39	3.11.39	Selly Park, B'ham
*Dennis Markham	29.5.32	Mrs Lively, Didbrook	11.9.39	3.11.39	Selly Park, B'ham
*Jean Markham	22.6.34	Mrs Lively, Didbrook	11.9.39	3.11.39	Selly Park, B'ham
*Jillian Brockwell	6.1.33	Mrs Severs, Didbrook	11.9.39	27.7.45	St Helier, Morden, London
Ronald Smith	11.7.31	Mrs Baker, Hailes	11.9.39	15.9.39	Oakley Rd B'ham
Doris Smith	8.8.34	Mrs Baker, Hailes	11.9.39	15.9.39	Oakley Rd, B'ham
*David Watkins	16.1.27	Mrs Turner, Coscombe	18.9.39	15.12.39	Sharman's Cross, B'ham
*Patricia Watkins	26.8.30	Mrs Turner, Coscombe	18.9.39	15.12.39	S Margaret's, Olton, B'ham
*Robert Aird	27.4.31	Mrs Archer, Didbrook	25.9.39	31.7.42	Upminster, Essex
*Mavis Caldicott	18.8.32	Mrs Bridges, Wood Stanway	2.10.39	15.11.39	Cotteridge, B'ham
June Wilkins	4.11.33	Name?, Church Stanway	30.10.39	28.11.39	B'ham
Dennis Cox	8.10.28	Mrs Archer, Didbrook	5.4.40	30.10 42	Hay Mills, B'ham
Reginald Cox	1.3.30	Mrs Stanford, Wood Stanway	5.4.40	19.12.41	Hay Mills, B'ham
Walter North	29.12.31	Mrs Cook, Hailes	5.4.40	1.5.40	Hay Mills, B'ham
Joseph Wall	21.6.29	Mrs J Wyniatt, Stanway	5.4.40	3.5.40	Hay Mills, B'ham
John Gosling	16.12.27	Mrs G Lively, Didbrook	5.4.40	19.12.41	Hay Mills, B'ham
Albert Hulbert	4.6.27	Mrs W Mann, Didbrook	5.4.40	12.6.42	Hay Mills, B'ham
Gordon Fuller	9.5.28	Mrs Hughes	5.4.40	4.9.42	Hay Mills, B'ham
Douglas Fuller	12.9.29	Mrs Hughes	5.4.40	4.9.42	Hay Mills, B'ham
William Garfield	18.3.30	Mrs A Wyniatt	5.4.40	5.4.44	Hay Mills, B'ham
Betty Vickery	15.1.30	Mrs Cross	5.4.40	9.1.42	Hay Mills, B'ham
Mary Cliffe	11.9.34	Mrs Simpson	5.4.40	17.4.40	Hay Mills, B'ham
Jean Humphreys	3.3.33	Mrs Roberts	5.4.40	15.5.42	Hay Mills, B'ham
Pamela Bradshaw	21.7.32	Mrs K Wright	5.4.40	13.3.42	Hay Mills, B'ham
Patricia Bradshaw	1.10.33	Mrs K Wright	5.4.40	13.3.42	Hay Mills, B'ham

Name	Date	Name/Address	Date	Date	Place
Victor Vickery	14.4.33	Mrs Cross, Church Stanway	20.5.40	2.2.44	Hay Mills, B'ham
Joan Vickery	27.8.31	Mrs Cross, Church Stanway	20.5.40	9.1.42	Hay Mills, B'ham
Marjorie Perren	4.10.29	Mrs Courage Farmcote	18.6.40	21.6.40	Hunter's Hall, Dagenham
Betty Cole	17.12.29	Mrs Courage, Farmcote	18.6.40	21.6.40	Hunter's Hall, Dagenham
*Diane Dally	12.7.32	Mrs Baker, Hailes	24.6.40	17.1.42	Gary's School, London
$*Mavis Caldicott	18.8.32	Mrs Bridges	1.7.40	20.6.41	Cotteridge, B'ham
$Walter North	29.12.31	Mrs Doddridge, Wood Stanway	10.7.40	13.5.43	Hay Mills, B'ham
Pamela Reed	14.12.28	Miss C Lane, Stanway	30.9.40	19.3.43	Eastbourne
Gladys Hopkinson	3.10.26	Mrs Holmes	30.9.40	1.11.40	Bourne Mod, Eastbourne
*Patricia O'Neill	2.6.28	Mrs Baker, Hailes	30.9.40	9.10.40	Plaistow, London
James Hopkinson	23.11.28	Mrs Holmes, Didbrook	30.9.40	29.11.40	St Mary's, Eastbourne
Derek Sharp	9.5.29	Rev Allen, Didbrook	30.9.40	29.11.40	West Ham or Eastbourne
George Caldicott	10.10.35	Mrs Bridges, Wood Stanway	30.9.40	20.6.41	Birmingham
Peter Savage	22.10.33	Mrs Stone, Hill Stanway	30.9.40	20.12.40	Forest Hill, London
Robert Potter	3.5.30	Rev Allen, Didbrook	30.9.40	2.8.43	Christ Church, Eastbourne
Jean Ashby	8.1.27	Col. Knight, Wood Stanway	30.9.40	22.11.40	St Saviour's Eastbourne
*Ethel Clarke	7.8.28	Mrs Edmonds, Church Stanway	30.9.40	28.10.40	Camrose Sen, Edgware, London
Douglas Reed	22.11.26	Miss C Lane, Stanway	7.10.40	22.8.41	Eastbourne
* Eileen Peckett	21.2.27	Mrs Hughes, Stanway	14.10.40	20.12.40	Willesden, London
*David Watkins	16.1.27	Henry Watkins, Taddington	28.10.40	10.4.41	Sharman's Cross, B'ham
David Ringshall	19.10.28	Mrs Courage, Farmcote	11.11.40	9.6.41	Eastbrook, Dagenham
Paul Ringshall	5.4.31	Mrs Courage, Farmcote	11.11.40	9.6.41	Hunter's Hall, Dagenham
*Barry Allen	14.4.28	Mrs Stone, Hill Stanway	19.11.40	21.3.41	Kings Heath, B'ham
*Garth Allen	15.1.35	Mrs Stone, Hill Stanway	19.11.40	4.7.41	Grendon Road, B'ham
Roderick Cooke	27.3.45	NK	25.11.40	25.4.41	Cherry Wood Rd, B'ham
Philip Cooke	6.2.30	NK	25.11.40	25.4.41	Cherry Wood Rd, B'ham
Gwendoline Potter	1.8.28	NK	25.11.40	16.10.41	Henson, Ramsgate
Bettina Potter	30.10.30	Mrs Fathers, Didbrook	25.11.40	16.10.41	Henson, Ramsgate
David Potter	6.7.33	Mrs Fathers, Didbrook	2.12.40	16.10.41	Henson, Ramsgate
David Pantlin	28.9.35	John Pantlin, Didbrook	9.6.41	17.6.41	Walton, Liverpool

Roy Bishop	16.9.36	Wood Stanway House	15.9.41	29.9.41	Eastbourne
$David Pantlin	28.9.35	At Didbrook	15.9.41	17.10.41	Liverpool
Malwyne Mallard	25.9.33	Didbrook Vicarage	28.5.42	2.7.42	Worthing
Leonard Garfield	21.3.33	JH Bowles, Wood Stanway	14.12.42	5.4.44	Birmingham
*Peter Stanford	2.1.34	William Bridger	27.3.44	19.9.45	St Mary's, Battersea, London
*Ann Bridger	27.2.38	William Bridger	27.3.44	28.11.45	St Mary's, Battersea, London
John Lock	25.11.38	Mrs Buttle, Church Stanway	25.5.44	9.7.45	Tulse Hill, London
Raymond Johnson	NK	Mrs Stanford, Wood Stanway	26.6.44	25.8.44	Balham, London
Phyllis Wilson	29.4.33	Mrs Bennett	9.8.44	6.10.44	Bexhill, Sussex
Sylvia Wilson	28.1.37	Mrs Bennett	9.8.44	6.10.44	Bexhill
Edward Wilson	13.6.35	Mrs Bennett	9.8.44	12.12.44	Bexhill
William Wilson	NK	Mrs Bennett	9.8.44	12.12.44	Bexhill
Eileen James	22.7.32	Mrs Holdsworth, Hill Stanway	9.8.44	4.10.44	Bexhill
David James	31.5.37	Mrs Holdsworth, Hill Stanway	9.8.44	4.10.44	Bexhill
Derek Rhodes	27.8.31	Mrs Peacock, Coscombe	25.9.44	4.10.44	Bexhill
Anthony Rhodes	23.11.33	Mrs Peacock, Coscombe	25.9.44	4.10.44	Bexhill
Gillian Carey	18.5.33	Didbrook Vicarage	4.12.44	14.12.44	Battersea, London
Alan Carey	25.8.37	Didbrook Vicarage	4.12.44	14.12.44	Battersea, London

*Unofficial evacuee

$See above (evacuated for a second time)

NK = Not Known

Notes: 22 children were not included on the Official evacuation list; their details were extracted from the school's admissions register.

Most of the evacuated children seem to have adapted well to living in the country with their hosts and made themselves at home. Many went back to their own homes once the worst of the blitz was over, some returned when the bombing increased again, others came later in the war, and a few stayed until the war was over (the records may be incomplete). In 2005, over 60 years from when he was evacuated from Balham, London, to Wood Stanway, Raymond Johnson paid a brief visit to Didbrook School. He described how he came with his mother and two of his mother's sisters and their two tiny babies to stay with his aunt, Mrs Stanford. They were made to feel very welcome, but caused great overcrowding in Mrs Stanford's small cottage. So the farmer, Mr Mann, arranged for them to have a cottage behind the farm and everyone was kind and helpful and they were given lots of pots and pans, furniture and bedding. Ray has very happy memories of his time there, including walking over the fields to school and in the evenings playing with the local children in the fields alongside their cottage and in the woods nearby. However, Glyn Wright recalls that the boys who were evacuated to Stanway formed a gang which he watched having major fisticuffs with a similar gang of evacuated boys living in Didbrook; Glyn kept out of the battle and is not clear who won or whether Raymond was among them!

The War Effort
Defence

On December 14th 1939, on receipt of instructions from the Secretary of State for Education about Air Raid Warnings, Mrs Holdsworth interviewed people in houses neighbouring the school and received promises from Mrs Archer, L Archer, A Wyniatt, W Jones and Rev HB Allen, each to receive a group of half a dozen children on receipt of an Air Raid warning - other children who could return home within 5 minutes were to do so.

On May 10th 1940 an Air Raid practice was held and gas masks were tested and adjusted. In February 1941 Mrs Holdsworth gave the senior children a demonstration of methods of dealing with an incendiary bomb, having received instruction herself.

I well remember how my mother, a trained nurse, was put in charge of the first aid post for Didbrook village. She invited all the women to our farm house and gave them instruction in the treatment of wounds and fractures and used me, lying on the sofa , as a 'patient' in need of bandaging, for the purpose of demonstration. I was fascinated and felt very important.

Fortunately these precautions were never required, as the village was never attacked. A single bomb was dropped in 1940 close to the railway viaduct near Toddington but fortunately this caused no damage or injuries.

Working for Victory

On May 24th, 1940, Empire Day, *'the union Jack Flag was flown and songs for our king, country and empire were sung. The Head Teacher gave a talk on the privileges and responsibilities of members of the British Empire. Children were also reminded of ways in which they can help during the present crisis - National Savings Stamps, collection of waste materials, knitting comforts etc.'*

On June 11th 1940 the first demonstration in a course of lecture-demonstrations on Wartime cookery was held in the schoolroom at 6.30 pm by a teacher of the Gloucestershire County Domestic Science Staff, and on February 11th 1943 Mrs Holdsworth accompanied the senior boys and girls to the first of four further demonstrations in Wartime Cookery arranged by the Local Education Authority at Stanway Memorial Hall. I attended one lecture in Stanway's Tithe barn with my mother. I remember being warned against using tinned foods if the cans were rusty or damaged, because of the risk of food poisoning. Tinned foods were new then to country housewives, who were used to having fresh meat, fruit and vegetables.

On July 4th 1941 the school closed for a fortnight's holiday for fruit picking. Mrs Holdsworth and Miss Last took parties of children to Hailes to pick redcurrants and 2,239 lb were gathered by the school. The school closed on August 22nd for 3 weeks' holiday, *'to be devoted whenever possible to the organised gathering of blackberries and elderberries for the (Toddington) jam factory'*. From September 16th there was a four day holiday to gather blackberries, elderberries and nuts in the Hailes plantation, with the teachers supervising groups of children. Also, from September 25th the afternoon timetable was altered to arrange parties for blackberrying, and for digging potatoes in the School Allotment. Over a month, on Mr Lesley Idiens' farm at Hailes, the children gathered 1,975 lb of blackberries and about a thousand pounds of elderberries for the jam factory. Also, at the end of October, Mrs Philpott accompanied a group of senior children potato lifting on Mr Austen Righton's farm at Stanway - truly digging for victory!

On September 4th 1942 the school closed for three weeks to pick blackberries and nuts and on September 30th the teachers accompanied groups of children gathering rose hips, to be made into Rose Hip Syrup for the Ministry of Food, and on October 2nd and 9th to gather horse chestnuts (in total 8 ½ cwt were obtained).

Children contributed to the war effort throughout 1943. May 22nd was the start of 'Wings for Victory week' during which pupils saved £207-7s-6d through the National Savings Group. Also, during the Whitsuntide holiday, the children collected 770 books for the National Salvage Effort. On July 2nd the school closed for two weeks during which the teachers organised parties of children to pick red currants at Hailes, in August school closed for a week for pea-picking, harvest and forestry and in September it closed for two weeks for harvest and *'nutting'*.

In 1944 school closed for 3 weeks on August 31st for nut picking and potato lifting.

Maintaining morale

Although some were excused military service because they were needed to work in agriculture to provide food for the nation, the fathers and other male relatives of many of the pupils were conscripted. Many unmarried young women were also called up. So the children were often brought up in difficult circumstances. Moreover, all the men remaining the village were expected to join the Home Guard and were often away on exercises at night. My mother was uncomfortable being left alone with three small daughters when my father was out at night, so her friend, Mrs Hilda Archer, whose husband was away in the army, often spent nights at the farm with her. Other young mothers and children in the village must have had similar anxieties.

A number of parties and other events helped to maintain morale. For example, on December 18th 1940 the staff and students of Miss Kerr-Sanders' Secretarial College, gave a the school children a Christmas party at Stanway House, which had been requisitioned to allow the College to be evacuated there from Kensington, London.

On September 3rd 1942, the pupils listened to a radio broadcast Service of Intercession on the 3rd anniversary of the outbreak of war.

The Home Guard

Front row: Hubert ('Boy') Hammett, Austen Righton, John Hyatt, Frank Mann, John Bourne, Leslie Idiens, William (Bill) Mann, Arthur Newman, unknown, Frank Vellender, Sydney Doughty

2nd row: William (Bill) Knight, Harry Fennel, Reg Turner, John Tysoe, Hubert Wynniatt, ? Fred Doughty, Michael Preston, Christopher ('Joyful') Vellender, Ernest Doddridge, Jim Hughes, Gilbert Wilcox, unknown

3rd row: unknown, Joe Hitchman, ? Steve Cook, unknown, Colin Holdsworth, Alfred Borley, unknown, Albert ('Gaffer') Edmonds, William Arthur Nightingale, ? Clark, ? Norton, Jim Wyniatt, Les Pullam

(photograph provided by Philip Mann)

On December 22nd 1943, the afternoon session at school finished at 3pm so that the children could go to a Christmas Party organised by the American Army troops who were in camp at Toddington Manor, where they had a vehicle depot. Glyn Wright remembers that all the children were given peanuts, their first experience of this delicacy, and a tin of chocolate powder to take home. Mrs Holdsworth was not very keen on the American GIs, who from time to time would march past the school and slip the pupils packets of chewing gum through the fence. She forbade the children to talk with them. Nevertheless, she accepted their invitation for the teachers and children to attend a Thanksgiving Day Party at Toddington Manor on November 23rd 1944, and took them there by bus. This outing was greatly enjoyed, as was the Christmas Party for the children and teachers held after school on December 19th 1944 at the Stanway Memorial Hall.

Victory

On May 8th and 9th 1945 there were two days holiday to celebrate the end of the war in Europe, and the unconditional surrender of Germany. Then, on May 10th at 11am there was a short service of thanksgiving in the school. The School Managers and Rev and Mrs Bidlake were invited to join this and Rev HB Allen gave a short talk. During the afternoon the children had games and a party, with milk, lemonade and buns.

There was also a victory celebration at Stanway House, which most of the children attended with their parents and many other people from the local villages. There were games for the children and a bonfire near the Pyramid, above the House, on which an effigy of Hitler was burned. The day finished with a dance in the Tithe Barn where, as so many men were still away on military service, most of the dancing was done, as described by Joyce Grenfell, 'bust to bust'.

On July 17th 1945 Mrs Holdsworth took the children by private bus to Winchcombe Cinema to see the film of the Victory Parade.

In contrast to the slaughter in the First World War, the only man from Didbrook Parish who was killed in the Second World War was Sergeant William Grove Spencer, RAF VR. Also, one of Mrs Alcock's grandsons, Oswald Culverwell, who had spent some of his childhood and school years at Didbrook School, was killed over Berlin at the age of 22 years when serving with the RAF VR. Two men from Stanway were killed, Lawrence John Samuel Bolton and Reginald Victor Turpitt, whose two young children, David and Rosemary Turpitt, were both pupils at Didbrook School.

After the War

Food rationing, which had started in January 1940 because over 50% of Britain's food was then being imported and the enemy was attempting to sink the ships bringing this, was not completely lifted until 1954. During and for some years after the war, fuel and clothing were also rationed. Many of the local population were working in agriculture under the direction of the County War Agricultural Executive Committee (The War Ag) to produce the food that the nation required and this situation continued for some time after the war. Most families in the local villages grew their own vegetables, many kept a pig and chickens, and the school children also did their bit. For example, on September 29th 1947 school closed early to allow the children to gather rose hips towards the national effort and 145 lb were sent to the collecting depot at Toddington.

On April 12th 1948 a large packing case of tinned jam, fruit, fish, jellies, sweets and other items was received at the school as a gift from Bramley School in Johannesberg, South Africa. The pupils wrote letters of thanks to Bramley School and on April 28th the children entertained the Old Age Pensioners of the parish to tea, to share the good things they had received. In July a large package of letters was received from the children of Bramley School. Also, a gift box was received during the summer holiday of 1948 from Oaonui School in New Zealand and on March 9th 1949 another large package of food was received from Bramley School.

Many years later, in 2007, as part of their lessons in history, the Juniors at Didbrook School re-enacted some of the aspects of World War II under the tutelage of their teacher, Graham Murray.

SOURCES

1.   War Memorials in Didbrook and Stanway Churches and at
      Stanway Crossroads
2.   Supplement to the London Gazette of Tuesday, 24th December,
      1918
3.   Admissions Register, Didbrook School
4.   Official evacuation list for Stanway Council School,
      Gloucestershire County Archives

Chapter 7.
CHILD HEALTH AND WELFARE

....And then the whining school-boy, with his satchel
And shining morning face, creeping like a snail
Unwillingly to school....

William Shakespeare (1564-1616), As You Like It, Act II

The law and school attendance

At the beginning of the 19th century school attendance was not obligatory and was not enforced as schools for the poor were still being established and child labour was required to support families' income and the needs of the Industrial Revolution. So the initial legislation aimed to reduce the working hours of children to provide at least a little time for education. Thus, Robert Peel's Factory Act of 1802 restricted hours worked by children to 12 a day and his Factory Act of 1815 restricted employment to children aged over 10 years. The 1833 Factory Act stipulated that children aged 13 to 18 years must not work more than 69 hours a week (12 each weekday and 9 on Saturdays), those aged 9 to 13 years were restricted to 48 hours per week (8 a day) while those aged less than 9 years were not to be employed. Children aged 9 to 13 were to attend schools provided by their employers for at least 2 hours a week. Sir James Graham's Factory Act of 1844 stated that children aged 8 to 13 should spend either 3 whole days or 6 half days per week at school. Their hours of work were limited to 6 ½ a day and they had 2d a week deducted from their wages to pay for their schooling [1].

Much of this early legislation related particularly to children living in towns. However, during the 19th and early 20th centuries children living in country areas were also essential members of the work force. The 1851 census described many children in Didbrook and Stanway, even as young as 8 years, as farm labourers or workers in other trades [2]. So the school holidays at Didbrook and Stanway Schools, which were scheduled by the local vicars, were arranged to allow children to provide the maximum possible help on the farms, particularly during hay-making, harvest and the fruit-picking seasons. If the weather led to early or late ripening of crops, the vicars would adjust school holiday dates accordingly.

Children's work included planting and picking up potatoes, thrashing corn, gleaning, gardening, gathering cowslips (probably to make wine) and harvesting the huge quantities of fruit that were required for the jam factory at Toddington, owned by the Tracy family. Children also helped with animal husbandry, *'bird keeping'* (presumably rearing pheasants and partridges for the shoots) and other agricultural tasks. Girls were often needed to care for their younger brothers and sisters at home, so that their mothers could go out to work. It is hardly surprising, therefore, that in the Parochial Returns for Didbrook, Hailes and Pinnock of 1818 it was recorded that only 20 children were attending the two day schools, whereas 61 were attending Sunday School [3].

As well as work, other rural activities also accounted for absences from school. Thus, Stanway School's Log Book records that on December 17th to 19th 1866 there was *'short attendance owing to Pheasant Shooting'*, on January 7th 1869 *'3 boys were absent for the purpose of acting as beaters for a shooting party'*, on 14th *'some gone with a foxhunting party in the neighbourhood'* and on 21st *'four boys away engaged as beaters for shooters'*.

Attempts to make school attendance obligatory were not successful and the 1870 Elementary Education Act aimed to improve this situation by creating School Boards which could provide new schools from the rates and pay fees for children of poor families. The Boards could make local by-laws for compulsory attendance of children aged between 5 and 13 years, but many did not. They could also fine parents for their children's non-attendance. In some areas children aged over 10 years who had passed Standard V were allowed to leave school [1].

Mr Mundella's Elementary Education Act of 1880 made school attendance compulsory from 5 to 13 years, except that children who had passed Standard V could leave at 10 years, as could any child who had completed a certain level of cumulative school attendance (the 'Dunce's pass') [1]. So in 1880, Mr Haslum, the School Attendance Officer *'took down the names of James Vakley 12 years - John Higgins 12 years - at work for farmers - both should be at (Didbrook) school'*. On September 20th 1880 the mistress of Stanway School sent out enquiries to the parents of four children who were absent. The replies were that two of the boys were still at work with the harvest and one little girl *'had not boots to come in'*. In 1881, a girl's attendance, despite Mr Haslum's cautions, remained so poor that her father was served with a summons, after which her attendance improved. But in 1882 the father of two

Stanway School children who had been served with a summons arrived at the end of the school day the worse for drink to complain that he had been fined 10 shillings. He said he should '*have them out*' and took his children home.

The Elementary Education Act (School Attendance) of 1893 raised the minimum school leaving age for all children to 11 years but, despite Mr Haslum's efforts, some children still left school prematurely. Thus, in 1898 Florrie Brooks was needed at home because her mother was ill. Although she had passed the examination for a labour certificate, she was only ten and was therefore denied permission to leave Didbrook School - but she stayed at home anyway, until she officially left when she was eleven.

In April 1901 a girl who had been working in service was brought back to Didbrook School by the Attendance Officer because, although she was 13, she had not passed the prescribed standard. There appears to have been some difficulty in interpreting the Bye laws which stated '*that a child must attend school between the age of 5 and 13*'. The new Attendance Officer, Mr Woodward, said that 14 was the age at which a child may leave school. Clearly hitherto many children had left before that age. Perhaps Mr Woodward was interpreting the Bye Laws differently from his predecessor, Mr Haslum. The matter was sent to the Board at Winchcombe for a ruling and meanwhile another 13 year old was refused permission to leave school.

The 1918 Education Act made education compulsory for all children aged 5 to 14 years, ie they could not leave until their 14th birthday [1] and made employment of children aged less than 12 years illegal. Children aged over 12 years could be legally employed on school days only before 6 am or after 8 pm and for 2 hours on Sundays, but not in factories, mines or street-trading.

The 1936 Education Act raised the school leaving age to 15 years, but implementation had to be delayed until after WW II as was also, in the Winchcombe area, the provision of separate schools for secondary education. The 1944 Education Act provided (in 1945) free secondary education for all and raised the school leaving age to 15, implemented in 1947 [1].

The last change to the school leaving age was to increase it to 16 years, which was implemented in 1972 [1].

Despite all these regulations, some country children continued to help with agricultural work throughout the 20th century and into the 21st century, albeit latterly mostly out of school hours.

Other Obstacles to School Attendance

Until well into the 20th century all the children had to walk to and from school. Some walked long distances, for example from Farmcote or Lynes Barn, respectively two and three miles from Didbrook, and so they were often absent especially in winter because of snow, or when there was heavy rain. In January 1881 two pupils of Stanway School had such severe chilblains that they could not attend school, as they could not get their shoes on, and in 1883 a child was away from Didbrook School for nearly 5 weeks because of '*chilled feet*'.

Illnesses, mostly resulting from infectious diseases, also accounted for many absences from school, as did 'industrial accidents' acquired by children doing agricultural work.

Illnesses

The epidemics recorded in Didbrook School's Log Books are shown in Table 9. Particular problems occurred in 1903, when there was gross overcrowding in Didbrook School due to the arrival of the children of the workers building the new railway line. By the end of the year nearly 100 children were crammed into the schoolroom. The railway children lived with their parents in huts near Toddington Station. The crowded conditions in the school and the huts would have facilitated the spread of streptococcal infections, which manifested as sore throat and a rash, called scarlatina. In some children these infections lead to rheumatic fever, with the potential to cause permanent damage to the heart. Dr George Cox, the local family doctor who was based at Winchcombe and was also Medical Officer of Health for the Area, ordered that none of the children from the Upper huts must attend school until this outbreak of streptococcal illness was over. There was also an epidemic of 'contagious eczema' (impetigo) among the railway children.

Smallpox had perhaps been the most feared infectious disease. It occurred in epidemics and had a high mortality. In 1796 Edward Jenner (1749-1823), who was a general practitioner in his native Gloucestershire village of Berkeley, discovered that pus taken from a cowpox vesicle on the skin of a milk maid, when inoculated into the skin of someone else, lead to an attack of cowpox, which was effective in preventing the more serious illness, smallpox, in the recipient. The introduction of immunisation against smallpox, ie vaccination using cowpox virus (cow = vacca in Latin) became routine and in Didbrook the School was used as the local vaccination centre. On April 18th 1882, and many times subsequently, the school was closed for half a day 'on account of public vaccination being held in the school room'. When on April 29th 1904 Nellie Williams from the Upper huts developed smallpox, only her immediate contacts in these huts were kept from school. Such was the efficacy of vaccination that not a single child at school or in the huts caught the infection (presumably the child with smallpox had never been vaccinated, whereas all the other children had been). However, many adults had still not been vaccinated so several workers developed smallpox and were nursed in the Isolation Hospital, Enfield Cottage, on Langley Hill above Winchcombe [4]. Nellie recovered and resumed school on June 20th. Some years later, in July 1923, there was a case of smallpox at Greet. Nurse Hunt called at the school and spoke to all the children about the benefits of vaccination, and on July 10th Dr Cox and Dr Pimm of Winchcombe came to the school and vaccinated 30 schoolchildren and 6 adults. Many of the children had very sore arms afterwards but none developed smallpox and clearly the important role of vaccination was by then well understood by the general population.

Another much feared infection was poliomyelitis, but there was only one mention of this in the two schools, in April 1919 when Annie Vellender was away from Stanway School suffering from 'infantile paralysis'.

There is a record that in April 1938 forms were received at Didbrook School for parents to sign consent to their children aged 2 to 8 years being immunised against diphtheria. This elicited a cautious response, only 11 of 22 parents agreeing to what must have been the first such immunisation programme in the Parish. However, in 1941 over 50 children were immunised, following the receipt of many evacuees.
But immunisations against most other infections were not available and so there were frequent epidemics, as shown in the table, which also shows the approximate dates when immunisation against them was introduced. On many occasions Dr Cox ordered that the school be closed to reduce spread of disease. Although the record of infections may be incomplete, it is evident that in the years after WW II, as routine immunisations were introduced, children lost much less schooling on account of epidemics.

Table 9.

INFECTIOUS DISEASES

Infection	Years in which the infection was recorded	Years when school was closed because of the infection	Approximate dates when immunisation began
Chicken pox (varicella)	1890, 1894, 1905, 1913, 1914, 1928, 1938, 1956, 1983	1905 - 6 weeks including holidays 1914 - 2 weeks	2002 (not given routinely)
Contagious eczema (impetigo)	1893 and many times subsequently	-	-
Diphtheria	1903 (Head mistress and her daughter affected)	1903 - 2 weeks	1940s
Influenza	1882, 1890, 1892, 1918, 1922, 1924, 1927, 1929, 1936, 1983	1918 - 2 weeks 1922 - 2 weeks 1927 - 2 weeks	1940s (mainly for the elderly and high risk groups)
Measles	1889, 1900, 1913, 1924, 1928, 1936, 1941, 1952	1889 - 4 weeks 1900 - 7 weeks 1924 - 1 week 1928 - 2 weeks	1960s
Mumps	1882, 1911, 1936	-	1950s
Ringworm	1893 and many times subsequently	-	-
Rubella (German measles)	1940, 1983	-	1970s
Scarlet fever (scarlatina or presumed streptococcal sore throat) and/or rheumatic fever	1889 (followed by rheumatic fever in one child), 1903 (followed by rheumatic fever in one child), 1910. In 1914 two girls had serious heart trouble (probably rheumatic fever) and a boy had rheumatism in 1915	1903	-
Smallpox	1904, 1923	-	1850s
Tuberculosis (consumption)	1903, 1915, 1960 (school cleaner)	-	1940s
Whooping cough (pertussis)	1880, 1883, 1904, 1908, 1911, 1922, 1929, 1933, 1953, 1982	1908 - 2 weeks 1911 - 4 weeks	1950s

It is likely that these records were incomplete

Until after WW II most of the cottages had outside privies and did not have a bathroom. Some did not even have a tap and the author remembers women in Wood Stanway fetching water in buckets and jugs from stand pipes in the street; the stone housings for these still exist. During the 1940s and 50s a programme to install modern bathrooms in most of the cottages, was followed by a great reduction in the reports of impetigo, ringworm and nits, presumably resulting from improved personal hygiene.

Accidents and Injuries

As well as his other duties, Dr Cox, set broken bones and undertook other surgical procedures, such as amputating fingers damaged in accidents (see below). He operated in his surgery or at Winchcombe Cottage Hospital, where children could be nursed afterwards. For example, in July 1890 Charles Fisher fell at a stile on his way to school and broke the 'splinter bone' of his leg. He was carried to school in a perambulator and from there by horse and trap to Winchcombe for treatment, and returned to school in September.

In October 1890 a boy from the infant class, Arthur Knowles, had an accident caused by putting his hand in a chaff cutter. He lost three fingers and was nursed in Winchcombe Cottage Hospital afterwards. Chaff cutters were used to cut straw, chaff, hay, and oats into small pieces before being mixed together with other forage and fed to horses and cattle. The early cutters had a knife resembling a guillotine which was driven up and down by a foot-operated treadle as the straw was pushed through. Subsequent models were turned manually, driven by steam, petrol-fuelled engines or electricity. There were no guards or rails on the early models to protect the operator and between 1890 and 1911 at least five young children attending Didbrook School lost or crushed fingers or thumbs while using them (Arthur Knowles, Maggie Fisher, Ernest Cook, Alfred Launchbury and Cecil James). Also, Albert (Bertie) Brooks cut both hands badly, but the cause was not described. Arthur Badcock cut his finger in a turnip cutter and Walter Wyniatt cut his finger so badly while chopping wood for his mother that Dr Cox had to remove it. Similar injuries were described in the Log Books of Stanway School: in 1880 James Collins injured one of his fingers which had to be amputated, in 1888 another little boy crushed his fingers badly, in 1889 a little boy had the end of his thumb cut off by a chaff cutter and, during the summer holidays of 1889, a third standard girl had two of her fingers taken off at the second joint with a hatchet.

A chaff cutter of a type used in Gloucestershire.
This example was photographed at Wormington,
by kind permission of Mr John Russell (JRM).

There were also a number of burn injuries. On November 5th 1897 Sydney Martin *'met with a serious accident through an explosion of gunpowder'* and was away from school for some time. On January 7th 1901, Matilda Parker, had a serious accident at school, caused by putting *'her foot on the top bar of the grate igniting her clothes. She was met at the door between the two yards which was fortunately open...... The flames were quickly but with difficulty smothered and the child who was badly burned was saturated with linseed oil, bound up, covered with a rug and taken in a neighbour's horse and trap to the Winchcombe Cottage Hospital.'* She did not return to school until February 28th. Mr Stanton, the vicar, said that a guard must be provided for the fire, and he arranged for Matilda to be provided with new clothes for when she came out of hospital, as all her clothes had been burnt. In February 1910 two children received burns: Willie Price accidentally scalded both legs at home and Henry James had his neck accidentally burnt at the Blacksmith's.

On December 17th 1947 during the afternoon recreation period, Sheila Nightingale, aged 13, put her arm through the glass window of the back door, causing a large wound. Mrs Holdsworth called a private hire car and took her to Winchcombe Hospital, where Sheila later had an anaesthetic for the insertion of 17 stitches.

On March 12th 1959 an infant fell while at school and cut his forehead; he and his mother were taken to Winchcombe Hospital by Rev G Bidlake, where Dr Shortt stitched the wound.

Child and adult mortality

Unfortunately premature deaths were common during the 19th century; the Registers of burials for Didbrook, Stanway and Hailes show that approximately half of all deaths then were in babies, children and young adults, presumably resulting mostly from poverty, poor housing and infectious diseases [5, 6, 7]. In 1859 three children from the Keyte family, who lived in Toddington, died within a period of 16 days, presumably from an infection. Several other families from Stanway, Didbrook and Hailes lost more than one child. In 1884 Mrs Alcock recorded that the doctor had advised that Edith Horlick should not attend Didbrook School more than half time because of her delicate health and shortly afterwards all the Horlick children were kept at home for a week because of the death of a little sister. Examples of tragic deaths at Stanway School included Mary Halling, who died in 1863 from '*water on the brain, following the measles*', William Turner, who was drowned in July 1880 and Emily Collett, who died in 1885 after being ill for about a year. On February 4th 1906 one of the Standard I pupils at Didbrook School, Mabel Lane, died of '*brain fever*', presumably meningitis.

Illness and death of parents often lead to severe consequences for their children. For example, in February 1900 Mrs Alcock recorded that '*the little Thornes*' attended school irregularly because of the illness and death of their father and in April two of them were sent to an orphanage. On March 20th 1903 she recorded that the three Dykes children were away at their mother's funeral and in 1910 that Mr Charles Horlick had died leaving four little children, who all attended the school. Details of how these two families managed after losing parents were not described.

However, Mrs Morna Fisher recalls that after her father, Horace Horlick, died suddenly of meningitis in 1926 aged only 47 years, leaving a widow Madeline and six children, the two older children, John and Mary, aged 15 and 14 years, left home to start, respectively, an apprenticeship with an uncle and a post as a lady's maid. Also, Madeline's sister, Mrs Millward, who had recently been widowed too, moved with her four children from Winchcombe to the Horlick's cottage at 69 Didbrook. Madeline then went to Mayfair in London to work as a lady's maid to support the family, leaving her sister to bring up her own and the four younger Millward children. Madeline was not able to return to Didbrook for about twenty years.

On November 13th 1903 there was a terrible Railway accident at Toddington. The Stanway viaduct was being constructed and, probably because the wooden supports were removed before the mortar joining the brickwork had fully set, four arches collapsed, bringing down a steam crane weighing 13 tons. Four men were killed and seven more were seriously injured by falling masonry [4, 8]. Many of children living in the Railway huts had a father or friends killed or hurt, and they stayed away from school for some time afterwards.

Deaths in the young gradually became less frequent during the 20th century, particularly after WW II, following the advent of antibiotics and immunisations. However, there were still occasional tragedies from accidents, such as the death on February 5th 1939 of Donald Nightingale, aged 7, who had accidentally drowned in a local pool. Mrs Holdsworth and senior children attended his funeral.

Preventive Medicine

From 1889 or earlier until the 1930s Dr Cox, paid occasional visits to Didbrook School, gave vaccinations and dealt with emergencies there, as did his successors after he retired.

The Education Act of 1907 [1] instituted a compulsory system of medical inspections in elementary Schools by school doctors, which probably started at Didbrook on June 25th 1909, when Dr Middleton Martin examined all the 22 children (of 57) who were at school that day. His successors included Drs S Wilson, Blake, Cameron, S Knight, Seacome, Gordon, Enid Clow, Cole, Fielden, KE Allen, Smith, Sloan, Roberts, Kloer, V Simon and Brooks.

There was also a school nurse who paid frequent visits. In April 1918 two mothers complained that their children had caught lice from other children. The District nurse, Nellie Hunt attended, examined every child and excluded two of them until their lice had been cleared. She was vigilant in examining the children to check for lice, ringworm and impetigo and arranged appropriate treatments; children were usually excluded from school until treatment was successful. Nurse Hunt's successors included Nurse Jenkins, Nurse Williams, who began visiting the school in 1931, Nurse ('nit nurse') Bailey who first came in 1932, Nurse Powell, Nurse Griggs, Nurse Renshawe (Health Visitor), Miss Bright (HV), Mrs Annan and Mrs Gregory. Also, in 1934 a County Health Visitor Miss McLauchlin, called to see a child with a speech defect and another with wry neck. Her successors made occasional visits as necessary for other problems.

One of the most important roles of the school nurse was to arrange immunisations. For example, on May 7th 1957 the District Nurse visited to arrange for children to be immunised against poliomyelitis and Dr Knight immunised other children in 1958. Injections against poliomyelitis were also given to 29 pupils on May 15th 1961 and in July 1962 (when there was a polio epidemic in Britain) two children were given oral polio vaccine.

Regular dental surveillance probably started in June 1919 when the school dentist inspected the teeth of 20 children and in July returned to treat 9 of them, assisted by Nurse Hunt. Over the years the school dentists included Mr Wren, Mr Willetts, Mr Crowther and Mr Merritt. Audiometric monitoring (tests of hearing) was also carried out from the 1960s onwards.

Poverty, social problems and crime

Both Didbrook and Stanway Schools operated under financial pressures, particularly before they were awarded Government grants. These were mitigated by, for example, the practice of selling the girls' needlework to augment school funds and in 1880 Mrs Alcock described how the school girls at Didbrook commenced sweeping and dusting the schoolroom 'instead of employing a woman'. The amounts awarded as Government grants were reduced if the attendance or academic attainment of the pupils was poor, so the head teachers and the Attendance Officer were vigilant in pursuing absentees.

Some parents were not able to afford the school fees for their children and there are a number of reports in Didbrook School's Log books of payment being provided by the Winchcombe Board of Guardians. The fees varied from 2 to 4 pence per child per week. In 1890 a mother wanted to keep her son away from Stanway School for two days, and the School's Log Book records that she complained that to have to pay 1½ d for the remainder of the week was too much, so she kept him away for the whole of the week.

Parents also had to pay for some of their children's books and Stanway School's Log Book records that in August 1882 a boy was sent home to get 8d to pay for 4 books, a sum that had been owing for nearly 12 months. He returned with a note saying *'Father says he can't make money, and you'll have to wait for it till the harvest'*. In this context it is relevant that most of the pupils were children of agricultural labourers, whose wages in the area in 1870 were approximately 10 shillings per week [9] rising slowly to only £1 18s 10d per week by 1939-40 [10]. Some of the more skilled workmen had additional 'hidden' income in the form of a tied cottage, in 1870 worth about 1s 6d per week [9]. The earnings of children, particularly of boys aged over 10 years, were therefore important to augment family income; in 1870 payment of about 10 shillings per month to each of two sons of workers on Ireley Farm was recorded [9].

By contrast, in 1870 the annual 'living' of the vicar of Didbrook was worth £257 [11] and in 1921 a farmer, Mr Mann, paid S Gobourn £12.12.0 for 'medical treatment', with Dr Cox being paid £2.13.6 'for attendance'; also a dental bill of £10.10.0 was paid to Mr Shovelton [12].

The Education Act of 1906 offered free school meals for the very poor [1] and from time to time throughout her headship Mrs Alcock provided hot food, such as soup, for children who came to Didbrook School without bringing anything for their lunch. She would also occasionally wash children who arrived at school in a dirty state. Even as late as 1932 the HMI's report about Didbrook School included *'a special word of praise is due for the care taken over the children who stay at school at midday. On two days of the week for the sum of 1d they are provided with a large bowl of nourishing soup'*.

In February 1891 Mrs Alcock recorded that a little girl was unable to attend Didbrook School *'for want of shoes'*, as was a child in July 1915 whose three siblings had been sent to school without dinner; they were taken into the school house and given a good meal. In September an Inspector from the Society for the Prevention of Cruelty to Children (SPCC) came and saw them because they had been reported as poorly nourished and clothed. On December 31st 1915 Mrs Alcock was asked to give evidence at the police Court in Winchcombe in the case of a prosecution against their mother in relation to her children's care. A child from another family was also away during October 1915 because she had no shoes. There were similar reports in the Stanway Log Books.

On October 8th 1937 a 6 year old girl arrived at School with an eye injured with glass from a broken window at home. Mrs Holdsworth *'telephoned the District Nurse, who said it was serious and that the child should go to hospital at once. As the child's mother is in hospital, I obtained a car and drove the child to the Cheltenham General Hospital, leaving the school in charge of Miss Last. The specialist said there was need for an immediate operation. The child remained in hospital while I visited the father, obtained his written consent and telephoned this message to the hospital. I returned to school 12.30. The Inspector of the NSPCC called at school to make enquiries re the......... children and my complaint of cruelty of the father towards .... aged 11'* (sister of the injured child).

Even as recently as the 1940s and 1950s many rural families lived in conditions of considerable poverty. For example, Glyn Wright, who left Didbrook School in 1946, remembers that even in winter children then walked from Farmcote or even further afield wearing only plimsolls, without socks, because their parents could not afford leather shoes or boots. When they arrived soaked through after walking through rain or snow Mrs Holdsworth washed the children's footwear and hung it on the fireguards around the stoves to dry.

On March 17th 1993 Mr Sanders attended a Case Conference in Tewkesbury about a pupil and a Child Protection order was issued and there may have been other occasions when child abuse or neglect was suspected, but these were not recorded in the Log books.

There are few records of children being in significant trouble with the law, although on April 22nd 1941 PC Smith called at the school to interview two boys who the previous evening started a fire that burnt down Mr Mann's barn and a thatched cottage. Minor acts of vandalism or other misbehaviour was generally managed by the local policeman and the head of the school. Nor was crime affecting the school premises a great problem. Once, on the evening of May 11th 1986, Mr Sanders received a telephone call from PC Collins to say that the school had been broken into, but that the thieves had already been arrested, in Prestbury. Keith and Nicky Gregory, who lived nearby had spotted them leaving the school, taken the number of their car and called the police. The thieves took the colour TV, a black and white TV (which the police subsequently returned) and some loose change. The offenders were subsequently convicted. In 1993 following another break-in, an intruder alarm system was installed.

SOURCES

1. Curtis SJ. History of Education in Great Britain, 7th Edition, University Tutorial Press, London, 1967
2. Census of 1851 accessed through AncestryLibrary.com
3. Education of the Poor. A Digest of Parochial Returns made to the Select Committee appointed to inquire into the Education of the Poor, Session of 1818, Vol 1, pages 321, 325 and 1464, ordered by the House of Commons, 1.4.1819. Public Records Office, Kew
4. Baker A and Abbott P. An Illustrated History of the Stratford on Avon to Cheltenham Railway, pages 17-20. Irwin Press, Oldham, 1994
5. Didbrook Parish Records: Registers of burials, 1813-2007
6. Stanway Parish Records: Register of burials, 1813-1998
7. Hailes Parish Records: Register of burials, 1813-20025
8. Maggs C and Nicholson P. The Honeybourne Line. The Continuing Story of the Cheltenham to Honeybourne and Stratford upon Avon Railway. Line One Publishing Ltd, Cheltenham, GL 50 3AA, 1985
9. Miller C. The account books of Thomas Smith, Ireley Farm, Gloucestershire 1865-71, pages xxx-xxxi. Bristol and Gloucestershire Archaeological Society, Alan Sutton Publishing Ltd, Gloucester, 1985.
10. Farm Account Books 1939-40, W Mann and Sons, Stanway, Gloucestershire.
11. Kelly's Post Office Directory, 1870.
12. Farm Diaries 1917-1927 written by William and Frank Mann, W Mann and Sons, Stanway, Gloucestershire.

Chapter 8.
ISBOURNE VALLEY SCHOOL

Between 2006 and the reopening of Didbrook and Toddington Schools as Isbourne Valley School in September 2008, much work was done by the Temporary Governing body to consider what changes were needed to bring about the amalgamation and to arrange for them to be carried out. The chairman was Mr Paul Workman and there were representatives of both Didbrook and Toddington Schools on the committee.

In the summer term and holiday of 2008 substantial renovation and redecoration of Toddington School was undertaken to make it suitable and safe for the Reception class and Infants (Years 1 and 2). This included provision of new toilets, moving the library, adapting an area as a computer room for the children, creation of a staff room, refurbishing the ceilings and lighting, upgrading the Security system and rebuilding the fences.

At Didbrook, which was to be used for the Juniors, little renovation of the building was required immediately, as there had been much recent work there, but telephone and IT networking were provided between the Didbrook and Toddington buildings. Also, following an act of vandalism in the grounds, a CCTV security system was installed in 2009.

A minibus was purchased to allow staff and pupils to be transported as necessary between the Didbrook and Toddington sites. Lord Wemyss generously allowed a piece of the orchard adjacent to Didbrook School to be fenced off and used as a parking area for the minibus and a car. There was already adequate parking space at Toddington. The minibus is used daily to transport to and from school the children of parents who do not drive, and/or have children attending both sites (there is no public transport available). It is also used to take groups of children to sports events with other schools in the area. Several members of staff and parents of pupils have taken the necessary MiDAS (Minibus Driver Awareness Scheme) test and now provide a rota of volunteer drivers.

The name for the new combined school was decided following a consultation process with pupils, parents and the governing body, and then a vote. Isbourne Valley School was the most popular suggestion and was agreed upon. A competition was held to design an appropriate logo; the winning design is illustrated on page 148. A new school uniform was also selected and a new prospectus and website were produced.

The staffing arrangements for Isbourne Valley School were discussed and it was agreed that the administrative base for the Head Teacher (Mrs Marriott) and her assistant would be in the more spacious Didbrook site. There would be three classes, one at Toddington for the Reception children and the Infants in Years 1 and 2. At Didbrook there would be two classes for the Juniors, one for Years 3 and 4 and the other for Years 5 and 6. At Toddington a full-time teacher was to be supported by a full-time higher level teaching assistant and a teaching assistant and at Didbrook there would be two full-time teachers and two part-time teaching assistants. Mrs Marriott was also to undertake teaching for one day a week. It was possible to fill all these posts from among the staff of the previous Didbrook and Toddington Schools. Additional part-time staff members were recruited on a sessional basis to provide instruction in music and PE, and a parent, Mr D Hayling, provided sports coaching on a voluntary basis.

Much work was done by the teaching and administrative staff during the summer holiday to ensure that all the necessary furniture, books and equipment were in place at Didbrook and Toddington for the start of the autumn term.

Isbourne Valley School opened on September 3rd 2008 with a total of 65 pupils, 7 in Reception, 22 in Years 1 and 2, 21 in Years 3 and 4 and 15 in Years 5 and 6. The children quickly adapted to their school and were proud of their new uniforms which the Governors had agreed to provide. The teachers all had to adjust their roles, either by teaching a different year group from before, and/or by teaching in a different classroom.

As well as the standard curriculum, after school Clubs were established where children could learn chess, football, cross country running, hockey, cricket, rounders and dance. The vicar of the United Parish of Toddington, Stanway and Didbrook with Hailes, Rev Nikki Arthy, and the Director of Music for the Parish, Mr Malcolm Foster, provided a weekly religious service in the school. In September 2010 the new vicar, Rev Michael Hand, added a weekly Bible Club, after school. The school is in the process of forging a link with schools in Husby Parish, Sweden, where Mrs Marriott and Mrs Poulton paid a visit during April 2010.

The introduction of Forest School has been a particular success and is led by Mrs Denise Churchill, who received special training in this topic. Forest School provides children with opportunities to explore the rural environment and is undertaken on land in or next to both the Didbrook and Toddington sites.   Under supervision, the children make dens, whittle wood, make and cook on camp fires and conduct other activities. Forest School was started with the younger children and later extended to the older ones.

The school has adopted the Creative Curriculum, whereby skills are taught through a theme. This enables staff and pupils to work together, for example, in 2010 they produced a 'Great Exhibition' of Victorian life

The new Governing body, which included some people who had been governors of Didbrook and Toddington Schools and also some new governors, had its first meeting on September 24th, 2008.   Mr Paul Workman was elected Chairman. A new Parent-Teachers Association was also set up and organised a huge barbeque and party to celebrate the end of the first year of Isbourne Valley School.

Isbourne Valley's first OFSTED inspection was carried out on March 9th, 2010 and the School was assessed as a 'Good' school. The pupils, staff, parents and governors were delighted with this outcome and are determined to carry on with their good work so that children living in the rural area of North Gloucestershire which it serves can continue to benefit from the enviable educational opportunities which the school provides.   They celebrated their success at the end of term barbeque held in the orchard adjacent to the school on July 23rd, 2010.

Mr Paul Workman, Chairman of the Governors, Isbourne Valley School (JRM)

Mrs Lesley Marriott, Headmistress, and Miss Catherine Newbury, infant teacher, at the school barbeque, July 2010 (JRM)

Ms Jackie Gommer, mother of four children at the school, in charge of the barbeque, helped by Richard Henrick (JRM)

Left Mr Darren Hayling, volunteer sports coach, and right Mrs Gaynor Alexander, who created the school's vegetable garden; both were governors of Didbrook School. In the centre is Mr Richie Alexander. (JRM)

Isabel Cornwall dancing at the barbeque, with Abby Tustin in the foreground to her right (JRM)

APPENDIX

Staff and Governors of Isbourne Valley School 2008-2010

Teachers
Mrs L Marriott (Head), Mrs L Poulton, Mrs S Brewin, Mrs L Wood, Mrs G Derrett, Miss C Watterston

Higher Level Teaching Assistant
Mrs N Webb

Teaching Assistants
Mrs D Churchill, Mrs M Podd, Mrs J Sherwood Miss S Green

Clerical
Mrs J Brooks, Mrs J Taylor, Miss B Redding,

Cleaners
Mrs D Porter, Mrs D Calcutt

NOTE Not all the above members of staff were employed throughout the period.

Governors of Isbourne Valley School 2008-2010
Mr P Workman (Chairman), Mr E Albutt, Mr R Allen, Mrs M Blake, Mrs S Brewin, Mrs J Burke, Mrs D Churchill, Mr A Fawcett, Mrs H King, Prof J Mann, Mrs J McFarlane, Mrs L Marriott, Lord Wemyss, Mrs L Poulton, Dr S Santos and Mrs H Ward.

SOURCE

Mrs Lesley Marriott

A SCHOOL IN THE COUNTRY

INDEX

A SCHOOL IN THE COUNTRY

About the author, Jillian R Mann, MB, BS (Lond), FRCP, Hon FRCPCH, DCH

Jillian Mann was brought up at Upper Farm, Didbrook and, like both of her parents, her uncle and her two sisters and brother, was a pupil at the village's school. After passing the 11 plus examination, she went to Pate's Grammar School for Girls at Cheltenham and from there to study medicine at St Thomas's Hospital Medical School, graduating from the University of London in 1962. She continued her training at St Thomas's Hospital and the Hospital for Sick Children, Great Ormond Street until 1967 and then at Birmingham Children's Hospital, where she began research on the care of children with leukaemia and other cancers. In 1972 she became a consultant paediatrician at Selly Oak Hospital Birmingham with sessions also at Birmingham Children's Hospital and she moved to the latter full time in 1979 as consultant paediatric oncologist. One of the first doctors in the UK to specialise in the care of children with cancer, her clinical and research work in this field was recognised by the award in 1997 of an Honorary Professorship in the School of Medicine of the University of Birmingham. She retired in 2002. Jillian always retained her 'roots' in the Cotswolds, visiting the family farm frequently throughout her life and retiring to the area, where she is active in the churches and other local activities and a governor of the village school.

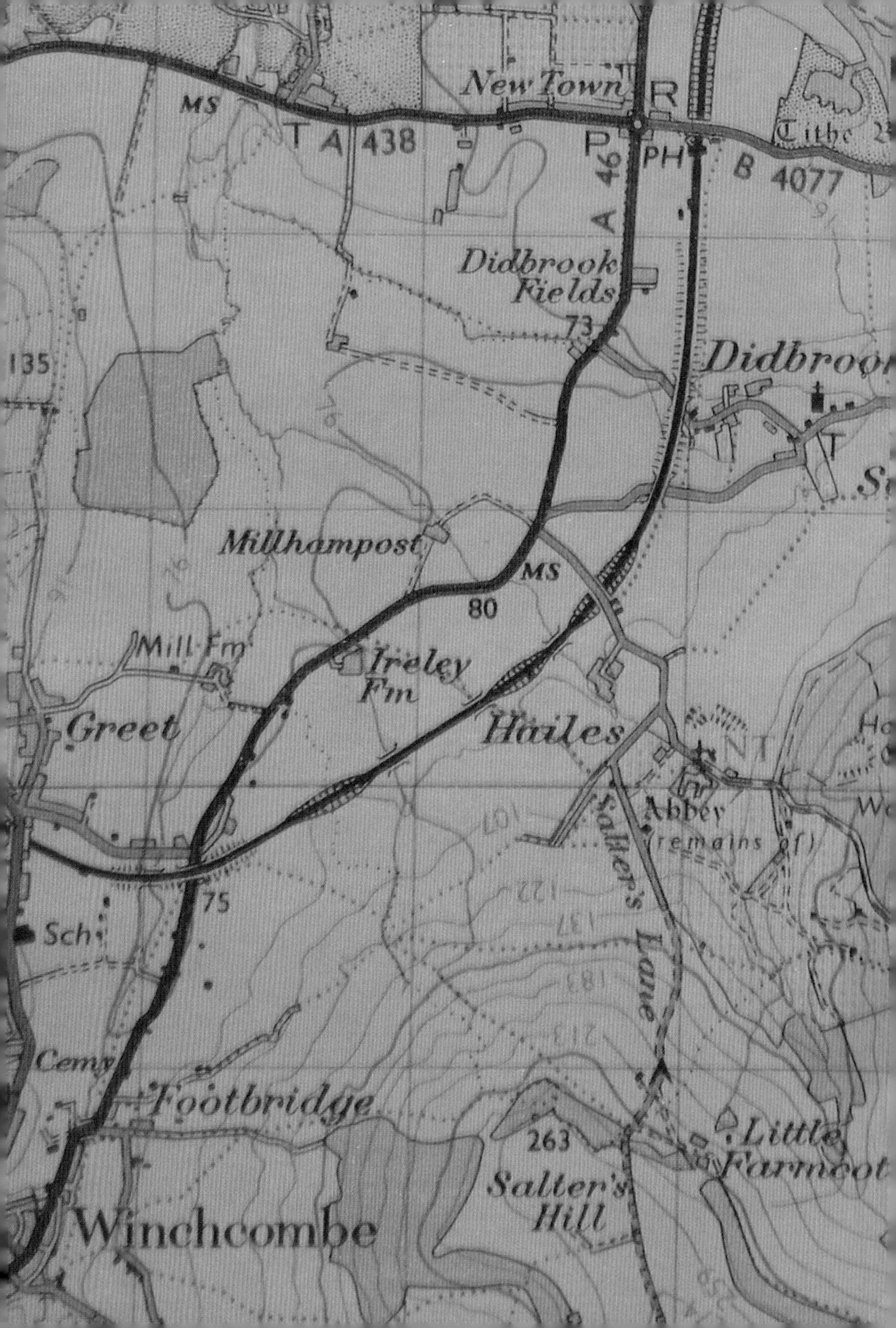

New Town

MS

TA 438

R
P

B 4077

Tithe

A 46

PH

Didbrook
Fields

73

Didbroo

135

T

S

Millhampost

MS

80

Mill Fm

Ireley
Fm

Greet

Hailes

Ho

107

Abbey
(remains of)

Wo

Salter's Lane

122

75

137

Sch

183

Cem

213

Footbridge

263

Little
Farmcot

Salter's
Hill

Winchcombe